Southern Living

the half-hour hostess

Hardcover ISBN-10: 0-8487-3608-7
Hardcover ISBN-13: 978-0-8487-3608-8

Softcover ISBN-10: 0-8487-3440-8
Softcover ISBN-13: 978-0-8487-3440-4
Library of Congress Control Number: 2010932899

Printed in the United States of America
First Printing 2011

OXMOOR HOUSE:
VP, Publishing Director: Jim Childs
Editorial Director: Susan Payne Dobbs
Brand Manager: Daniel Fagan
Senior Editor: Rebecca Brennan
Managing Editor: Laurie S. Herr

THE HALF-HOUR HOSTESS:
Editors: Susan Hernandez Ray, Katherine Cobbs
Project Editor: Holly D. Smith
Senior Designer: Melissa Jones Clark
Director, Test Kitchen: Elizabeth Tyler Austin
Assistant Directors, Test Kitchen: Julie Christopher, Julie Gunter
Test Kitchen Professionals: Wendy Ball, Allison E. Cox, Victoria E. Cox, Margaret Monroe Dickey, Allison Moreland Haynes, Callie Nash, Kathleen Royal Phillips, Catherine Crowell Steele, Ashley Strickland, Leah Van Deren
Photography Director: Jim Bathie
Senior Photo Stylist: Kay E. Clarke
Associate Photo Stylist: Katherine Eckert Coyne
Assistant Photo Stylist: Mary Louise Menendez
Senior Production Manager: Greg A. Amason

CONTRIBUTORS:
Designer: Blair Gillespie
Copy Editor: Rhonda Richards
Proofreader: Lauren Brooks
Photo Stylists: Missie Crawford, Lydia DeGaris Pursell, Mindi Shapiro Levine
Photographers: Van Chaplin, Beth Hontzas, John O'Hagan, Mary Britton Senseney
Indexer: Mary Ann Laurens
Interns: Christine T. Boatwright, Caitlin Watzke

SOUTHERN LIVING:
Executive Editor: Rachel Hardage
Food Director: Shannon Sliter Satterwhite
Senior Food Writer: Donna Florio
Senior Food Editors: Shirley Harrington, Mary Allen Perry
Senior Recipe Editor: Ashley Leath
Assistant Recipe Editor: Ashley Arthur
Test Kitchen Director: Rebecca Kracke Gordon
Test Kitchen Specialists/Food Styling: Marian Cooper Cairns, Vanessa McNeil Rocchio
Test Kitchens Professionals: Norman King, Pam Lolley, Angela Sellers
Senior Photographers: Ralph Anderson, Jennifer Davick
Senior Photo Stylist: Buffy Hargett
Assistant Photo Stylist: Amy Burke
Studio Assistant: Caroline Murphy
Editorial Assistant: Pat York

To order additional publications, call 1-800-765-6400 or 1-800-491-0551.

For more books to enrich your life, visit oxmoorhouse.com

To search, savor, and share thousands of recipes, visit myrecipes.com

Front cover: Shrimp-Pesto Pizza, page 179

Back cover (from left to right): Fast Fajitas and Southwestern Salad, page 128; Thai Noodle Salad, page 22

Southern Living®

the half-hour hostess

All Fun, No Fuss: Easy Menus, 30-Minute Recipes,
and Great Party Ideas

featuring **Rebecca Kracke Gordon**

Oxmoor
House®

table of contents

Let's get this party started...
the *Half-Hour Hostess* way!

It's easy to do! Armed with a few quick and flavorful recipes and a couple of clever ideas for your setup, you can put together a memorable party for family and friends in no time. Mix an upbeat attitude with a simple game plan, and you have the recipe for a fun event that guests will remember long after the party is over.

Learn how easy it is to become the consummate hostess. See how simple and fun it is to host parties that your friends and family look forward to with excitement. Entertaining isn't rocket science. It's as simple as deciding what type of party you'd like to throw. A birthday bash? A fireside supper for friends? A kids' pool party? You're only limited by your imagination! Need some inspiration? Here you'll find 35 menus for virtually every occasion. After you settle on a party theme, follow the "Hostess Hit List," my step-by-step plan for putting it all together in record time. Each menu has been carefully crafted to include delicious recipes that can all be prepared in a mere 30 minutes or even made well in advance of the appointed hour. "Time Shaver" notes show you how to streamline prep by utilizing store-bought ingredients when you're pinched for time.

There's more to a fun gathering than food and drinks—the best hostess pays attention to the details. From the invitations and place settings to the centerpieces and favors, it's the little things that give a party its unique vibe. Get inspired with page after page of beautiful, full-color photography showcasing unique party ideas. "Fast Flourish" tips sprinkled throughout the chapters illustrate the clever tricks that the *Southern Living* party experts have discovered over the years. "Quick Finds" provide helpful resources for locating ingredients and accessories. When there just isn't time to cook, look to the "Hostess Helper" tips that give you sneaky shortcuts to buying and embellishing great food. It's never hip to be square, so when you need an etiquette primer or an appropriate party favor idea, look to the **"Hip Tip"** boxes scattered throughout.

So let's party!

Rebecca Kracke Gordon

Rebecca Kracke Gordon
Southern Living Half-Hour Hostess

"Create your own party pantry by filling an old hutch with entertaining essentials. It's not only functional, but it's handsome too."

the Origin
of the *Half-Hour Hostess*

She loved to throw a great party, but it seemed, more and more, that she couldn't find the time with all that was on her plate. It was too much work, too time-consuming, too stressful. She liked things just so, and if she couldn't do it right, she just wouldn't do it at all. So alas, she went into social seclusion, venturing out to meet friends at coffee shops or restaurants instead. But something was missing. Her inner hostess was screaming to get out. She wanted to make time with her friends and family memorable. So she let down her guard, managed her expectations, and devised a plan to make party-giving fun again…and with that, the *Half-Hour Hostess* was born.

Why We Entertain

Southerners, by nature, are serial socializers. Blame the heat for this communal habit. It forced our great grandparents outside to seek a breeze on the porch while sipping iced tea or a spirited cocktail, and that often led to impromptu gatherings of neighbors and passersby.

The porch gave way to air-conditioned dining rooms, and planning a sit-down affair might take weeks. Save-the-date cards and invitations would be sent. Place settings and centerpieces were painstakingly arranged and the menus were designed to impress. Exhausted yet?

While the urge to entertain remains (by now it must surely be imprinted in our genes), the thought of hosting a party is intimidating. In our busy lives, it just seems easier to connect anywhere but at home. It doesn't have to be.

It's time to get the party re-started! Toss aside the formalities, and forget weeks of planning. Entertain 21st-century style! What's old is new again…welcome the return of the impromptu get-togethers that started it all on those porches long ago. If it's Thursday morning and you have an itch to have the girls over tomorrow night, go ahead and make some calls, and send some e-mails…make it happen! You can host a fun and festive gathering with minimal effort.

"Single stems are standouts in individual bud vases."

The *Half-Hour Hostess* is loaded with great ideas for throwing fun, simple parties of every kind. All you need are a few easy decorating tricks, a flourish or two added to store-bought items, and some from-scratch recipes that can either be made ahead or in 30 minutes or less. When your guests arrive you will be able to relax and mingle, which is the reason you planned the get-together in the first place, right?

Need a decorating idea on the fly? You'll find 12 "Fast Flourish" tips to inspire you. Looking for unique serving ideas or memorable party favors? Check out the "Hip Tips" throughout. Rebecca's "Hostess Helper" tips provide recipe shortcuts and time-saving secrets. "Quick Finds" notes give you great resources for ingredients, decorating items, and party favors.

Get ready to entertain the *Half-Hour Hostess* way!

Find Your Inspiration

You don't need an excuse to throw a party. But often it helps to build upon a theme. Perhaps it's a favorite color, the pattern of a pillow, a book you're reading, or a hit song. Let a single idea inspire you. Let those groovy tangerine plates you inherited from Aunt Barb dictate your color scheme, and run with it. Buy a dozen orange Gerber daisies and arrange them in stemless wine glasses down your buffet table for a bright, cheery display. Wrap napkins around silverware, and tie them with orange ribbon. Voila! Your decor is done. It will make an impact.

If spring fever has you pining for fun, invite friends over for a seasonal supper to wave the winter doldrums goodbye. Arrange flowering branches from your backyard in an old watering can. Think double-duty, and create place cards and take-home favors in one. Purchase a flat of pansies at the corner nursery and inexpensive mini terracotta pots. Personalize each pot with a guest's name and then plant with a pansy. It'll be the good time that keeps on giving.

Menu Planning

On the pages ahead, you'll find lots of great menus. When creating your own, there are a few things to keep in mind. It is important to vary tastes, textures, and colors for interest. You don't want your guests' plates to be monochromatic and drab. Keep things lively and bright. Include vegetarian and meat or seafood offerings so that there is something for everyone to enjoy. Contrast textures and temperatures for interest and to make your job easier. Pair a smooth, creamy dip with something crunchy. Serve warm grilled flank steak with a cool dressed salad. Please palates, and you will please guests.

Shopping

A well-stocked pantry is a hostess's best friend. With go-to entertaining staples always on hand, party prep is a cinch. Jarred olives, oil-packed sundried tomatoes, crackers, pesto sauce, roasted red peppers and canned beans are just a few of the many store-bought items that can be whipped into fantastic nibbles. Highly perishable items such as seafood should be purchased the day of the party. Prep any ingredients that you can the day before so that the day of the party, it's assemble-only.

Let Go

The best hostesses never panic when things don't go as planned. At the end of the day, it's really all about being with friends. If the flowers wilt, the wine is corked, and the soup boiled over, shrug it off. Great memories can be made over bottles of beer and a bowl of nuts as easily as bad ones can be made at swanky cocktail parties. It's really all about loving the ones you're with. Entertaining the *Half-Hour Hostess* way gives you more time to do just that.

cozy
gatherings

Entertaining an intimate crowd is easy.
Hone your hostess skills by throwing a
relaxed, impromptu get-together for your
closest friends.

girls' night in

menu

serves 4 to 6

Won Ton-Wrapped Fried Shrimp

Thai Noodle Salad

Asian Pork Wraps

chilled ginjo sake

gingersnap cookies

Time to send out party invitations to your girlfriends, or easier yet, text messages. Pass around Won Ton-Wrapped Fried Shrimp while everyone catches up over drinks. Turn your living room coffee table and floor cushions into the seating-and-eating area to enjoy an exotic feast. The success of the party will have your guests suggesting that "girls' night in" should become a recurring event.

hostess
hit list:

Doing the bulk of preparations the day before frees you up for your "dish de résistance"— the Won Ton-Wrapped Fried Shrimp. While they drain and cool a bit, simply toss the salad.

The day before:

- Prepare vermicelli for salad; cover and chill
- Make dressings for noodles and wraps; cover and chill
- Prep and chill veggies for noodles and wraps

30 minutes before:

- Wrap Won Ton-Wrapped Fried Shrimp
- Make Asian Pork Wraps

15 minutes before.

- Fry shrimp
- Toss together Thai Noodle Salad

Just before serving:

- Plate the dishes
- Give a toast, and clink glasses

Won Ton-Wrapped Fried Shrimp

makes 6 appetizer servings   hands-on time: 30 min.   total time: 30 min.

Be ready to serve these jumbo appetizers right when your guests arrive. Better yet, engage them in the cooking.

Vegetable oil

12 unpeeled, jumbo raw shrimp (16/20 count)

¼ cup bottled sweet chili sauce

1 Tbsp. soy sauce

2 Tbsp. minced fresh cilantro

1 tsp. red curry paste

1 garlic clove, minced

12 won ton wrappers

1 egg white, lightly beaten

1. Pour oil to depth of 2 inches into a Dutch oven; heat to 365°. Peel shrimp, leaving tails on. Devein, if desired.

2. Stir together sweet chili sauce and soy sauce. Combine cilantro, red curry paste, and garlic.

3. Brush one side of each won ton wrapper with egg white. Spread ¼ tsp. cilantro mixture in center of each wrapper. Top with one shrimp. Fold wrapper around shrimp; leave tail exposed, and press wrapper to seal. Brush outside of each wrapper with egg white.

4. Fry won ton-wrapped shrimp, in small batches, 2 to 3 minutes or until golden, turning once. Drain on a wire rack over paper towels. Serve immediately with sweet chili-soy sauce mixture.

Note: Won ton wrappers can be found in the produce section.

fast flourish Shop your **yard** for flowering or leaf-covered **branches** or even bare ones with architectural interest for a decidedly **Zen** feel.

"I like to use small bowls for sauces or to float delicate blooms in water. They look pretty without taking up too much room.**"**

Thai Noodle Salad

makes 4 to 6 servings   hands-on time: 25 min.   total time: 25 min.

1   (8-oz.) package vermicelli
⅓   cup chopped fresh cilantro
2   garlic cloves, minced
1   jalapeño pepper, seeded and chopped
¼   cup fresh lime juice
1   Tbsp. fish sauce*
1   Tbsp. honey

1½ tsp. sesame oil
¼   tsp. salt
2   carrots, grated
1   cucumber, peeled, seeded, and thinly sliced
1   cup finely shredded cabbage
¼   cup chopped fresh mint
¼   cup chopped dry-roasted peanuts

1. Prepare pasta according to package directions. Drain, rinse, and place in a large bowl.
2. Process cilantro and next 7 ingredients in a food processor until smooth, stopping to scrape down sides.
3. Toss together pasta, cilantro dressing, carrots, and next 3 ingredients. Sprinkle with peanuts, and serve immediately.
*Soy sauce may be substituted.

Time Shaver: Substitute ¾ cup bottled Thai dressing instead of making your own (omit cilantro through salt).

quick finds Ginjo or "premium" **sake** can be found at most liquor stores and is best served slightly chilled.

fast flourish Let the food be your centerpiece. If you don't have time to make the wraps, arrange components of the dish artfully in unique containers to create a self-service station.

Asian Pork Wraps

makes 8 servings   hands-on time: 15 min.

total time: 15 min.

Save time in the kitchen by picking up pork from a local barbecue joint.

¾   cup low-fat sesame-ginger dressing
2   Tbsp. creamy peanut butter
1   tsp. dried crushed red pepper
1   lb. shredded barbecued pork without sauce*
¾   cup dry-roasted peanuts, coarsely chopped
8   (10-inch) burrito-size flour tortillas
1   head napa cabbage, shredded (about 8 cups)
1   (11-oz.) can mandarin oranges, drained
3   green onions, sliced
2   Tbsp. chopped fresh cilantro
2   Tbsp. chopped fresh mint

1. Whisk together sesame-ginger dressing and next 2 ingredients until smooth.
2. Drizzle half of dressing mixture over pork, tossing to combine. Stir in peanuts.
3. Place tortillas between damp paper towels. Microwave at HIGH 45 seconds; keep warm.
4. Place cabbage and next 4 ingredients in a large bowl; drizzle with remaining half of dressing mixture, tossing to coat.
5. Spoon about ½ cup pork mixture and ½ cup cabbage mixture just below center of each tortilla. Fold bottom third of tortillas up and over filling, just until covered. Fold left and right sides of tortillas over, and roll up.
*1 lb. shredded cooked chicken may be substituted.
Note: We tested with Newman's Own Lighten Up Low Fat Sesame Ginger Dressing.

so happy
it's friday with friends

menu

serves 12

Mint Juleps

Crostini bar

Warm Olive Sauté

Spicy Pickled Shrimp

Celebrate the weekend with your best pals at home. The evening's signature cocktail, Mint Julep, sets a Southern tone. A menu that's based on make-ahead nibbles from pickled shrimp to dressed-up pimiento cheese crostini means less time in the kitchen before your guests arrive.

hostess
hit list:

Get a jump-start on the food the day before, so when you get home from work, it's a matter of reheating and assembly. Set up a tray on a chest or table to create a bar and to catch condensation from chilled cups. You'll need a jigger to measure the bourbon plus stirrers and fresh mint sprigs for serving.

The day before:

- Make Cornbread Crostini; cover and chill in an airtight container
- Make Warm Olive Sauté; cover and chill
- Make Spicy Pickled Shrimp; cover and chill
- Make mint syrup for juleps; cover and chill
- Fill bud vases with flowers

30 minutes before:

- Reheat Cornbread Crostini and Warm Olive Sauté
- Embellish pimiento cheese (see "Hostess Helper")

15 minutes before:

- Top crostinis
- Spread crackers with pimiento cheese
- Arrange food on platters and in bowls

Just before serving:

- Light candles; play music
- Fill ice bucket with crushed ice
- Make Mint Juleps individually as guests arrive

crostini with tomatoes, Cheddar cheese, mayonnaise, and bacon

Cornbread Crostini topped with Gorgonzola cheese, apples, and parsley

pimiento cheese on crackers

Mint Juleps

makes 16 servings   hands-on time: 5 min.   total time: 20 min.

2   cups sugar
1   (1-oz.) package fresh mint, torn
Bourbon

Club soda (optional)
Garnish: fresh mint sprigs

1. Bring sugar and 2 cups water to a boil in a small saucepan, and cook, stirring constantly, 1 minute or until sugar dissolves. Remove from heat. Add torn fresh mint. Let stand 10 minutes. Pour through a wire-mesh strainer into a decorative pitcher; discard solids.

2. Pour mint syrup over ice into 16 (12-oz.) julep cups (2 Tbsp. each). Fill cups with bourbon and, if desired, a splash of club soda. Garnish, if desired.

Cornbread Crostini

makes 5 dozen   hands-on time: 15 min.   total time: 30 min., not including cooling

Top these hearty bites with Gorgonzola cheese crumbles, apple slices, and parsley sprigs. For 12 servings, you'll need 1 apple, 1 cup Gorgonzola cheese, and ¼ cup fresh parsley sprigs.

2   cups self-rising white cornmeal mix
2   cups buttermilk
½   cup all-purpose flour

2   large eggs, lightly beaten
¼   cup butter, melted
2   Tbsp. sugar

1. Preheat oven to 400°. Stir together all ingredients just until moistened. Spoon batter into greased muffin pans (about 1 Tbsp. per cup). Bake 15 minutes or until golden brown.

Make Ahead Note: Cool completely, and freeze in zip top plastic freezer bags up to 1 month. To serve, arrange cornbread rounds on a baking sheet, and bake at 350° for 5 to 6 minutes or until thoroughly heated.

hostess helper For the crostini bar, rely on quality, store-bought ingredients whenever possible. Here we topped purchased crostini with **plum tomato slices,** shredded **Cheddar cheese,** crumbled **bacon,** and a dollop of mayonnaise. We gussied up deli **pimiento cheese** with a pinch of smoked paprika, spooned it on crackers, and garnished with sliced chives. Homemade Cornbread Crostini is the star with its Gorgonzola cheese and apple topping.

Warm Olive Sauté

makes 12 servings   hands-on time: 10 min.   total time: 16 min.

1   lemon
1   tsp. minced garlic
¾   tsp. fennel seeds
½   tsp. dried crushed red pepper
⅓   cup extra virgin olive oil

1½ cups mixed olives
8   pickled okra, cut in half lengthwise
1   fennel bulb, cored and sliced
½   cup roasted, lightly salted almonds

1. Remove peel from lemon, reserving lemon for another use. Sauté lemon peel, minced garlic, fennel seeds, and dried crushed red pepper in hot oil in a large skillet over medium heat 1 minute. Add olives, pickled okra, sliced fennel, and almonds. Cook, stirring occasionally, 5 to 7 minutes or until fennel is crisp-tender.

Spicy Pickled Shrimp

makes 12 servings   hands-on time: 23 min.   total time: 23 min., plus 1 day for chilling

For a shortcut, purchase already peeled and deveined shrimp.

2   lb. unpeeled, large raw shrimp (26/30 count)
3   small white onions, thinly sliced
½   cup olive oil
¼   cup tarragon vinegar
2   Tbsp. pickling spices
2   tsp. salt

1   tsp. sugar
1   tsp. Worcestershire sauce
½   tsp. dry mustard
¼   tsp. ground red pepper
¼   cup chopped fresh parsley

1. Peel shrimp; devein, if desired.
2. Cook shrimp in boiling water to cover 3 to 5 minutes or just until shrimp turn pink; drain. Rinse with cold water.
3. Layer shrimp and onions in a large bowl. Whisk together oil and next 7 ingredients; pour over shrimp and onions. Cover and chill 24 hours, stirring occasionally. Stir in parsley just before serving.

> "For a last-minute table decoration, I pick up some fresh flowers from the floral section of the grocery store and arrange them in a collection of colorful vases."

guys' game night

menu

---

serves 6 to 8

Mexican beers with lime wedges

Spicy Queso Dip

Two-Ingredient Guacamole

Black Bean Salad

Loaded Nachos

Keep the fun close to home the day of the big game by serving up a chip-and-dip feast sure to make sports fans swoon. Wooden plates won't break, and dark-colored napkins camouflage stains. Arrange the food on the coffee table and side tables so it's in easy reach of "in-the-zone" couch potatoes. Serve ice-chilled beer in a large galvanized tub resting on a towel-lined tray. Make sure there's an opener and, of course, a stack of cocktail napkins at the ready for dribblers.

hostess
hit list:

A chip-and-dip spread is a win-win for your sports fanatics and for the hostess, too! A little prep the day before the game will allow you to enjoy kick-off with the rest of the bunch.

The day before:

- Brown sausage for the queso; chill
- Place spinach for queso in refrigerator to thaw overnight
- Cook corn for the salad, and chill
- Make salad without avocado, and chill
- For the nachos, make sour cream mixture and cook meat mixture; chill separately
- Gather serving pieces and coolers

30 minutes before:

- Ice down beer
- Set up coolers
- Set up serving pieces

15 minutes before:

- Reheat nacho meat mixture in microwave; assemble nachos
- Prepare queso

Just before serving:

- Gently stir chopped avocado and corn into salad
- Make Two-Ingredient Guacamole

> **"** 'Keep it easy' is my motto for great fixin's without a lot of fuss...embellished, store-bought queso dip becomes downright decadent with a handful of add-ins! **"**

Spicy Queso Dip

makes 7½ cups   hands-on time: 15 min.   total time: 15 min.

2   (16-oz.) containers refrigerated hot queso dip
1   (16-oz.) package mild ground pork sausage
1   (10-oz.) package frozen chopped spinach, thawed
      and well drained

1   (15-oz.) can black beans, drained
1   (10-oz.) can diced tomatoes and green chiles,
      undrained
Tortilla chips

1. Microwave queso dip according to package directions in a 2-qt. microwave-safe bowl.
2. Meanwhile, cook sausage in a large skillet over medium-high heat, stirring often, 8 minutes or until sausage crumbles and is no longer pink. Drain.
3. Stir sausage, spinach, and beans into queso. Drain tomatoes and green chiles, reserving juice. Add tomatoes and green chiles to dip. Stir in enough reserved juice for desired consistency (about 2 to 3 Tbsp.). Serve hot with tortilla chips.
Note: We tested with Gordo's Refrigerated Hot Queso Dip.

quick finds Non-electric, stainless steel **thermal trays** keep things hot or cold thanks to an inner gel core. Find them at bed-and-bath chain stores or online. Simply heat or chill the tray according to the directions, and foods will stay at the ideal temperature much longer.

Two-Ingredient Guacamole

makes 2½ cups   hands-on time: 5 min.   total time: 5 min.

2   (8-oz.) packages refrigerated guacamole   Tortilla chips
¾   cup refrigerated salsa

1. Stir together both ingredients. Serve immediately with tortilla chips.
Note: We tested with Wholly Guacamole and Garden Fresh Gourmet Jack's Special Medium Salsa.

Black Bean Salad

makes 6 to 8 servings   hands-on time: 20 min.   total time: 20 min.

Stir in avocado just before serving if you don't plan to dig in right away.

3   ears fresh corn
3 to 4 Tbsp. lime juice
2   Tbsp. olive oil
1   Tbsp. red wine vinegar
1   tsp. salt
½   tsp. freshly ground pepper

2   (15-oz.) cans black beans, drained and rinsed
2   large tomatoes, seeded and chopped
3   jalapeño peppers, seeded and chopped
1   small red onion, chopped
1   avocado, peeled, seeded, and chopped
¼   cup loosely packed fresh cilantro leaves

1. Cook corn in boiling water to cover 5 minutes; drain and cool. Cut kernels from cobs.
2. Whisk together lime juice and next 4 ingredients in a large bowl. Add corn, black beans, and remaining ingredients; toss to coat. Cover and chill until ready to serve.

"Buy an assortment of blue and yellow tortilla chips, and toss them together for interest. Be sure to place several bowls around the room for easy dipping."

Black Bean Salad

Loaded Nachos

makes 4 to 6 servings   hands-on time: 27 min.   total time: 27 min.

With this full menu, one recipe should be enough to serve a crowd, but double the recipe and make two platters-worth of nachos if your guests are extra hungry.

¼ cup sour cream
2 Tbsp. bottled salsa
1 lb. lean ground round
1 cup chopped onion (about 1 medium)
½ cup chopped green bell pepper
1 cup bottled salsa
1 Tbsp. chili powder

2 tsp. ground cumin
¼ tsp. salt
6 cups tortilla chips
1 cup shredded iceberg lettuce
1 cup chopped tomato (about 1 medium)
1 cup (4 oz.) shredded sharp Cheddar cheese
¼ cup pickled jalapeño pepper slices

1. Combine sour cream and 2 Tbsp. salsa in a small bowl; stir well. Cover and chill until ready to serve.

2. Cook beef, onion, and bell pepper in a large nonstick skillet over medium-high heat, stirring often, 8 minutes or until beef crumbles and is no longer pink. Drain well; return meat mixture to skillet. Stir in 1 cup salsa, chili powder, cumin, and salt; bring to a simmer over medium heat, and cook 3 minutes.

3. Place chips on a large serving plate; top with meat mixture, lettuce, tomato, cheese, and jalapeño slices. Drizzle sour cream mixture over each serving.

hip tip Win fans' stomachs and hearts by not only serving up taqueria-inspired fare, but also by keeping beers cold with team-colored **koozies** that can be taken home after the game. Fill a bowl with lime wedges, and nestle it in ice so that drinks are easy to grab, garnish, and go.

toppings

panini party

menu

serves 6 to 8

Dressed-Up Tomato Soup

Cuban-Style Panini

Hot Brown Panini

Peppery Turkey-and-Brie Panini

orange slices

sweet potato chips

store-bought cookies

Fire up the panini press for your next get-together. Either assemble sandwiches ahead and grill them as guests arrive, or let your guests concoct and grill their own. The recipes that follow work well with either setup. From a zesty Cuban classic and famous Southern specialty to a decidedly gourmet combination of turkey and Brie, there is a panini for every palate.

hostess
hit list:

Let your guests create fabulous sandwiches with a build-it-yourself panini bar. Offer a variety of meats, breads, condiments, and cheeses, then marvel at the creative sandwiches that emerge from the press.

The day before:

- Prepare Dressed-Up Tomato Soup; cover and chill
- Purchase deli meat
- Purchase bread from deli or bakery
- Arrange ingredients for each sandwich on platters. Cover and chill.

30 minutes before:

- Prepare cheese sauce for Hot Brown Panini
- Slice oranges

15 minutes before:

- Prepare bread for panini
- Reheat soup
- Cook the bacon for the Hot Brown Panini

Just before serving:

- Place the sweet potato chips in a basket lined with a pretty napkin
- Set out toppings for soup and panini

Dressed-Up Tomato Soup

makes about 11 cups   hands-on time: 15 min.   total time: 15 min.

1 (28-oz.) can Italian-seasoned diced tomatoes
1 (32-oz.) container chicken broth
1 (26-oz.) can tomato soup

½ tsp. freshly ground pepper
Toppings: croutons; chives; chopped fresh parsley, basil, or rosemary; freshly grated Parmesan cheese

1. Pulse tomatoes in a food processor 3 to 4 times or until finely diced. Stir together tomatoes and next 3 ingredients in a Dutch oven. Cook over medium heat, stirring occasionally, 10 minutes or until thoroughly heated. Serve with desired toppings.
Note: We tested with Progresso Diced Tomatoes with Italian Herbs.

Cuban-Style Panini

makes 8 servings   hands-on time: 18 min.   total time: 18 min.

Turkey and roast beef add extra meatiness to this delicious spin on a traditional Cuban sandwich.

8   (3-oz.) white sub rolls, split
8   Tbsp. yellow mustard
8   dill pickle sandwich slices
12 oz. thinly sliced deli roast turkey

12 oz. thinly sliced deli ham
12 oz. thinly sliced deli roast beef
12 (1-oz.) Swiss cheese slices
¼   cup olive oil

1. Spread cut sides of each roll with mustard. Layer bottom halves of rolls with pickle slices and next 4 ingredients; top with remaining roll halves, pressing sandwiches together gently. Brush outsides of rolls with olive oil.
2. Cook sandwiches, in batches, in a preheated panini press 2 to 3 minutes or until golden brown.

hip tip Follow one of our recipes, or set up your own panini bar (see photo on page 40). Suggested bruschetta toppings: basil pesto • sun-dried tomato pesto • sun-dried tomatoes • fresh basil • fresh mozzarella • roasted red and yellow bell peppers • artichoke hearts.

> "Wrap sandwiches in parchment paper before grilling to keep your panini press clean. You'll still get the nice grill marks without a cheesy mess to clean up."

Hot Brown Panini

makes 8 servings   hands-on time: 28 min.   total time: 28 min., not including sauce

Piled high with chicken, White Cheese Sauce, bacon, and Swiss, Hot Brown Panini lends grilled goodness to this fresh take on a Louisville classic.

2   Tbsp. melted butter
16 (½-inch-thick) Italian bread slices
Parchment paper
1   cup (4 oz.) shredded Swiss cheese

3   cups chopped cooked chicken or turkey
4   plum tomatoes, sliced
White Cheese Sauce, warmed and divided
13 cooked bacon slices, crumbled

1. Brush melted butter on 1 side of 16 bread slices. Place slices, butter sides down, on parchment paper.
2. Sprinkle 1 Tbsp. Swiss cheese on each of 8 bread slices; top with chicken, tomato slices, and 1 cup warm White Cheese Sauce. Sprinkle with bacon and remaining Swiss cheese, and top with remaining bread slices, butter sides up.
3. Cook sandwiches, in batches, in a preheated panini press 2 to 3 minutes or until golden brown. Serve with remaining 2 cups warm White Cheese Sauce for dipping.

white cheese sauce

makes 3 cups   hands-on time: 20 min.   total time: 20 min.

Keep sauce warm in a 1.6-qt. mini slow cooker while sandwiches are grilling. Look for them at supercenters.

¼   cup butter
¼   cup all-purpose flour
3½ cups milk
1   cup (4 oz.) shredded Swiss cheese

1   cup grated Parmesan cheese
½   tsp. salt
¼   tsp. ground red pepper

1. Melt butter in a heavy saucepan over low heat; whisk in flour until smooth. Cook, whisking constantly, 1 minute. Gradually whisk in milk; cook over medium heat, whisking constantly, until mixture is thickened and bubbly. Whisk in cheeses, salt, and red pepper, whisking until cheeses are melted and sauce is smooth.

Peppery Turkey-and-Brie Panini

makes 8 servings   hands-on time: 18 min.   total time: 18 min.

1   (15-oz.) Brie round
16 multigrain sourdough bread slices
2   lb. thinly sliced smoked turkey

½   cup red pepper jelly
2   Tbsp. melted butter

1. Trim and discard rind from Brie. Cut Brie into ½-inch-thick slices. Layer 8 bread slices with turkey and Brie.
2. Spread 1 Tbsp. pepper jelly on 1 side of each of remaining 8 bread slices; place, jelly sides down, onto Brie. Brush sandwiches with melted butter.
3. Cook sandwiches, in batches, in a preheated panini press 2 to 3 minutes or until golden brown.
Note: We tested with Braswell's Red Pepper Jelly.

hostess helper If you'd like to add an appetizer to the menu, liven up store-bought **hummus** with black pepper and a drizzle of olive oil; serve with a gorgeous array of vegetables for dipping—pre-cut carrot and celery sticks, grape tomatoes, and broccoli and cauliflower florets.

fireside supper

menu

serves 6

Sweet Potato Soup

Peppered Beef Fillets with Pomegranate Jus

buttered orzo pasta

Rosemary Roasted Grape Tomatoes

Ambrosia Trifle

Take advantage of the first brisk nights of fall to invite friends to share a feast by the warmth of the fire. Layer the table with tablecloths or throws in autumnal jewel tones. Blankets on the backs of chairs let folks know it's time to hunker down and get comfortable over a leisurely dinner with friends. Wow them with an elegant menu that only you know took little time to make.

hostess
hit list:

It's amazing how easily this elegant menu comes together. The side dish, dessert, and soup can all be made ahead, and the main attraction cooks at the last minute.

The day before:

- Prepare trifle; cover and chill
- Make orzo; cover and chill
- Gather linens and tableware
- Prepare soup; cover and chill

30 minutes before:

- Prepare beef fillets
- Light the fire, torches, and candles

15 minutes before:

- Roast the tomatoes
- Reheat soup, and prepare garnishes

Just before serving:

- Reheat the orzo in microwave
- Pour the wine
- Put another log on the fire

Sweet Potato Soup

makes 6 cups   hands-on time: 15 min.   total time: 15 min.

Ground red pepper adds a spicy kick to this soup. You can prepare and chill the soup a day or two ahead, if you'd like. Just reheat it in the microwave, in a slow cooker, or on the cooktop.

1   (40-oz.) can yams in heavy syrup
1   (14-oz.) can vegetable or chicken broth
½   cup fresh orange juice
1   to 2 Tbsp. minced fresh ginger

1½ cups coconut milk
1   tsp. salt
¼   tsp. ground red pepper (optional)
Garnishes: croutons, ground red pepper

1. Drain yams, reserving ½ cup syrup. Discard remaining syrup. Place yams in a blender or food processor. Add ½ cup syrup, broth, orange juice, and ginger. Process 2 to 3 minutes or until smooth, stopping to scrape down sides.

2. Pour pureed mixture into a medium saucepan. Stir in coconut milk and salt. Cook over medium heat, stirring often, until soup is thoroughly heated. Ladle soup into bowls. Drizzle additional coconut milk into soup, if desired. Garnish, if desired.

Note: We tested with A Taste of Thai Coconut Milk.

hip tip Scented or citronella **candles** can overwhelm the senses while dining. Use **hurricanes** to shield unscented candles from the wind for a flickering ambience.

Peppered Beef Fillets with Pomegranate Jus

makes 6 servings   hands-on time: 22 min.   total time: 25 min.

The 1-inch thickness of the fillets is important for uniform cooking. Press fillets with the palm of your hand to make fillet thicknesses match.

¼ cup extra virgin olive oil

1 tsp. salt, divided

1½ tsp. freshly cracked pepper

1 tsp. dried parsley flakes

1 tsp. dried oregano

1 large garlic clove, pressed

6 (8-oz.) beef tenderloin fillets (about 1¼-inch thick)

⅔ cup minced shallots

⅔ cup refrigerated pomegranate juice or dry red wine

3 oz. crumbled Gorgonzola or blue cheese

1. Combine olive oil, ¼ tsp. salt, and next 4 ingredients. Sprinkle fillets with remaining ¾ tsp. salt, and rub with 3 Tbsp. olive oil mixture.

2. Cook beef in a large nonstick skillet over medium-high heat 5 minutes on each side or to desired degree of doneness. Remove fillets from skillet, and keep warm.

3. Add remaining 1 Tbsp. olive oil mixture to skillet. Add shallots, and sauté 2 to 3 minutes, stirring to loosen particles from bottom of skillet. Add pomegranate juice. Bring to a boil, and cook 1 minute.

4. Pour pomegranate jus over beef, and top with cheese.

fast flourish Gather fall leaves or pick up flats of plants with seasonal fall foliage or blooms, and insert into a florist foam wreath form for an autumnal display.

Rosemary Roasted Grape Tomatoes

makes 6 servings   hands-on time: 5 min.   total time: 12 min.

These tiny tomatoes take on a sweetness when roasted. Serve them as a simple side dish, or toss them with hot cooked pasta.

3   pt. grape tomatoes
1½ Tbsp. chopped fresh or dried rosemary
1½ Tbsp. olive oil

¾   tsp. salt
¾   tsp. freshly ground pepper
Garnish: fresh rosemary sprigs

1. Preheat oven to 475°. Rinse tomatoes, and pat dry with paper towels.
2. Combine tomatoes and next 4 ingredients; toss gently to coat. Place tomatoes in a single layer in a shallow roasting pan.
3. Bake at 475° for 7 to 8 minutes or until tomato skins are blistered and start to pop, stirring once. Garnish, if desired.

Ambrosia Trifle

makes 10 to 12 servings   hands-on time: 15 min.   total time: 25 min.

Layer these ingredients in one big bowl or several small hurricane glasses that each hold two servings. This makes enough for a big crowd, so you're sure to have leftovers the next day.

1   cup sweetened flaked coconut
1   (5.1-oz.) package vanilla instant pudding mix
1   (8-oz.) container frozen creamy whipped topping, thawed

2   (24-oz.) jars refrigerated mandarin oranges
½   (40-oz.) bakery pound cake, cut into 1-inch cubes

1. Preheat oven to 350°. Place coconut on a baking sheet. Bake 8 minutes or until lightly browned.
2. Meanwhile, prepare pudding according to package directions. Stir together pudding and 1½ cups whipped topping. Drain oranges, reserving liquid.
3. Layer half of cake cubes in 6 (2-cup) glasses or a 3-qt. glass bowl or trifle dish. Brush cake cubes with half of reserved liquid from oranges; spoon half of pudding over cubes. Top with half of oranges. Repeat layers, ending with oranges. Dollop with desired amount of whipped topping; sprinkle with toasted coconut. Chill until ready to serve.
Note: We tested with Del Monte Sun Fresh Mandarin Oranges.

Ambrosia Trifle

summer grill
get-together

menu

serves 6

Honey Tea

Flank Steak

Radish Salsa

grilled veggies

Italian Herb Bread

Grilled Banana Splits

Summertime is all about relaxing and enjoying the outdoors, so bring
the party outside too! Grilling is a great way for the cook to strut her
stuff and still be in the mix, plus you won't heat up the kitchen with this
menu that comes together almost entirely on the grill.

hostess
hit list:

Think "dessert first" when cooking, because it requires starting with a cold grill and a lower temperature. Plus you can rest assured that your impressive finale won't pick up the strong flavors of the main meal.

The day before:

- Make tea (omit ice)
- Slice desired vegetables for grilling
- Toast coconut and pecans for sundaes
- Pre-scoop ice cream and frozen yogurt

30 minutes before:

- Make Radish Salsa
- Grill bananas and pineapple
- Grill flank steak
- Grill desired vegetables alongside steak

15 minutes before:

- Grill bread
- Slice steak
- Set table; gather serving pieces
- Place ice cream and yogurt scoops in bowls— return to freezer until you're ready for dessert

Just before serving:

- Warm chocolate sauce
- Set up sundae/banana split bar

Honey Tea

makes about 2 qt.   hands-on time: 10 min.   total time: 25 min.

4 cups water

7 green tea bags

½ cup honey

4 cups cold water

1 navel orange, cut into wedges

1 lime, cut into wedges

1. Bring 4 cups water to a boil in a medium saucepan; add tea bags. Boil 1 minute; remove from heat. Cover and steep 10 minutes. Remove and discard tea bags.

2. Stir in honey. Pour into a 2½-qt. pitcher; stir in 4 cups cold water and orange and lime wedges. Serve over ice.

Note: We tested with Bigelow Green Tea.

Flank Steak

makes 6 servings   hands-on time: 21 min.   total time: 26 min., not including salsa

Flank steak is an inexpensive, quick-cooking cut that's loaded with flavor, making it a hostess favorite.

1 (2-lb.) flank steak

1 Tbsp. Montreal steak seasoning

Radish Salsa (optional)

1. Preheat grill to 350° to 400° (medium-high) heat. Sprinkle both sides of steak with seasoning. Grill steak, covered with grill lid, 8 minutes on each side or to desired degree of doneness. Remove from grill, and cover steak with aluminum foil; let stand 5 minutes. Uncover and cut steak diagonally across the grain into thin slices. Serve with Radish Salsa, if desired.

Note: We tested with McCormick Grill Mates Montreal Steak Seasoning.

radish salsa

makes about 2 cups   hands-on time: 10 min.   total time: 10 min.

6 large radishes, grated

1 large cucumber, peeled, seeded, and chopped

¼ cup chopped fresh cilantro

1 garlic clove, pressed

1 Tbsp. fresh lime juice

¼ tsp. salt

1. Toss together all ingredients. Cover and chill up to 2 hours, if desired. Season with salt to taste.

Italian-Herb Bread

makes 6 servings   hands-on time: 15 min.   total time: 15 min.

6   (1-inch-thick) Italian bread slices
2   Tbsp. olive oil
1   tsp. dried Italian seasoning

½   tsp. kosher or table salt
½   tsp. freshly cracked pepper

1. Preheat grill to 350° to 400° (medium-high) heat. Brush 1 side of each bread slice with olive oil; sprinkle with Italian seasoning, salt, and pepper. Grill bread slices, seasoned sides down, covered with grill lid, 4 to 5 minutes or until toasted.

Time Shaver: Frozen garlic-and-herb bread loaves can be wrapped in foil and heated on the grill. Just slice to serve.

hip tip Many vegetables are delicious **grilled**—asparagus, squash, eggplant, and mushrooms. Slice large vegetables lengthwise or crosswise to a uniform thickness. Toss them with a little **olive oil, salt, pepper,** and a sprinkling of **fresh herbs**. Grill and serve, or refrigerate and bring back to room temperature, when it's time to eat.

Grilled Banana Splits

makes 6 servings   hands-on time: 15 min.   total time: 30 min.

Choose baby bananas (also known as Oritos, Lady Fingers, and Manzanos) or small bananas that are just ripe but still firm so they'll hold their shape on the grill.

Vegetable cooking spray

¼ cup chopped pecans

¼ cup sweetened flaked coconut

6 unpeeled baby or small bananas with green tips*

6 fresh pineapple slices**

1 pt. vanilla ice cream

1 pt. chocolate frozen yogurt

Jarred chocolate topping, warmed

Garnish: maraschino cherries

1. Coat cold cooking grate of grill with cooking spray. Preheat grill to 300° to 350° (medium) heat.

2. Preheat oven to 350°. Place pecans in a single layer in a shallow pan. Place coconut in a single layer in another shallow pan. Bake pecans and coconut 7 to 8 minutes or until toasted and pecans are fragrant, stirring occasionally.

3. Peel bananas, and cut in half lengthwise. Coat bananas with cooking spray. Grill pineapple slices, covered with grill lid, 4 minutes on each side or until lightly caramelized. Grill banana halves 1 to 2 minutes on each side or until lightly caramelized.

4. Chop grilled pineapple. Arrange 2 grilled banana halves in each of 6 (8-oz.) banana-split dishes or other serving bowls. Scoop ¼ cup vanilla ice cream and ¼ cup chocolate frozen yogurt into each dish between banana slices. Top each with 1 Tbsp. chocolate sauce, 1 chopped pineapple slice, 2 tsp. pecans, and 2 tsp. coconut. Garnish, if desired. Serve immediately.

*3 regular bananas, peeled and quartered, may be substituted. Increase grilling time to 4 minutes on each side.

**Canned pineapple slices in juice, drained, may be substituted.

Note: If using a charcoal grill, place banana slices around the outer edge of grill to prevent burning. Watch them carefully, as they will cook fast. We tested with Smuckers Chocolate Dessert Topping.

hostess helper **Prescooped ice cream** and **yogurt** make banana splits a cinch. Place parchment-lined baking sheets in your freezer for 30 minutes. Place scoops onto cold pan, one by one, and freeze until firm. Cover with plastic wrap until you're ready to serve.

fast flourish Nestle colorful bowls brimming with scoops of ice cream in larger, ice-filled bowls in contrasting hues for an abundant spread that's as hardworking as it is good-looking.

catfish fry

menu

---
serves 6 to 8

Classic Fried Catfish

deli coleslaw

Shrimp-and-Okra Hush Puppies

Key Lime Pie

iced tea

A good old-fashioned fish fry is about as Southern as it gets. Tender catfish, plump shrimp, and okra are a deep fryer's best friends. Take this tasty idea, and roll with it. Enameled colanders lined with newspaper to absorb excess grease can hold the entire meal and have handles for portability. Finish with a refreshing, palate-cleansing slice of Key lime pie.

hostess
hit list:

Frying doesn't have to be a feat for the cook. The key is to fry in stages, keeping the first recipe warm in an oven while you fry the second.

The day before:
- Shop your home office for rubber bands and name tags
- Put name tags on glasses now so that they'll stick
- Bundle silverware
- Line colanders with paper
- Bake pie; cover and chill

30 minutes before:
- Prepare the Shrimp-and-Okra Hush Puppies; keep warm in oven
- Prepare the catfish; keep warm

15 minutes before:
- Put on some zydeco music
- Garnish pie

Just before serving:
- Spoon up the coleslaw, and pour the tea

Classic Fried Catfish

makes 6 to 8 servings   hands-on time: 25 min.   total time: 25 min.

For an extra-crispy crust, use stone-ground yellow cornmeal, if available.

Vegetable oil
1   cup plain yellow cornmeal
⅓   cup all-purpose flour
1¼ tsp. ground red pepper

½   tsp. garlic powder
2½ tsp. salt
12 catfish fillets (about 3¾ lb.)

1. Pour vegetable oil to depth of 2 inches into a Dutch oven; heat to 350°.

2. Combine cornmeal, next 3 ingredients, and 2 tsp. salt in a large shallow dish. Sprinkle catfish fillets with remaining ½ tsp. salt, and dredge in cornmeal mixture, coating evenly.

3. Fry fillets, in batches, 5 to 6 minutes or until golden; drain on paper towels.

Shrimp-and-Okra Hush Puppies

makes about 2½ dozen   hands-on time: 22 min.   total time: 27 min.

You'll need 10 oz. unpeeled shrimp to prepare this recipe.

1   cup self-rising yellow cornmeal
½   cup self-rising flour
1   cup peeled, medium-size raw shrimp, chopped
1   tsp. Creole seasoning
½   cup frozen diced onion, red and green bell pepper,
    and celery, thawed

½   cup frozen cut okra, thawed and chopped
1   large egg, lightly beaten
¾   cup beer
Canola oil

1. Stir together cornmeal and flour in large bowl until combined.

2. Sprinkle shrimp with Creole seasoning. Add shrimp, onion mixture, and okra to cornmeal mixture. Stir in egg and beer just until moistened. Let stand 5 to 7 minutes.

3. Pour oil to depth of 2 inches into a Dutch oven; heat to 350°. Drop batter by level tablespoonfuls into hot oil, and fry, in batches, 2 to 2½ minutes on each side or until golden brown. Drain on a wire rack over paper towels; serve immediately.

Note: Keep fried hush puppies warm in a 225° oven for up to 15 minutes. We tested with McKenzie's Seasoning Blend for diced onion, red and green bell pepper, and celery.

Key Lime Pie

makes 8 servings   hands-on time: 10 min.   total time: 20 min., not including cooling and chilling

Be sure to make the pie the day before the party so it has plenty of hands-off time to cool and chill for pretty slices.

1   (14-oz.) can sweetened condensed milk
¾   cup egg substitute
½   cup fresh Key lime juice
2   tsp. lime zest (about 2 limes)

1   (6-oz.) ready-made graham cracker crust
1   (8-oz.) container frozen whipped topping, thawed
Garnishes: lime wedges, lime zest

1. Preheat oven to 350°. Process first 4 ingredients in a blender until smooth. Pour mixture into piecrust.
2. Bake at 350° for 10 to 12 minutes or until golden. Let pie cool completely (about 1 hour). Cover and chill 3 to 24 hours. Top with whipped topping. Garnish, if desired.

"The office supply store can be a great source for the hostess. Rubber bands come in many colors and can be used for bundling silverware. Name tags can be used on canning jars to identify each guest's drink. You get the idea.**"**

hostess helper When Key limes are in season, squeeze the juice and freeze it in ice cube trays. Transfer the cubes to a zip-top plastic bag so you have a supply on hand.

backyard picnic

menu

serves 8

Chunky Sour Cream Dip with corn chips and carrots

Basil Egg Salad on Sourdough

Black-eyed Pea and Veggie Salad

PB & Chocolate Pan Cookies

Kick off your heels, spread a big blanket on the lawn, and tote dinner
outdoors for a low-key, casual meal shared with family or friends under
the floating clouds or twinkling stars. Drugstore-counter classics such
as egg salad sandwiches and marinated bean salad make this gathering
a fuss-free breeze.

hostess
hit list:

This make-ahead menu is perfectly portable when packed with care. Reach for containers with lids, takeout boxes, and parchment paper, and arrange them in a wicker basket with ice packs or into a cooler with wheels.

The day before:

- Prepare sour cream dip; cover and chill
- Make egg salad; cover and chill
- Make Black-eyed Pea and Veggie Salad; cover and chill
- Prepare cookie and let chocolate cool; cover

30 minutes before:

- Assemble and wrap sandwiches
- Cut cookie into triangles; cover

15 minutes before:

- Cut carrot sticks for dip and put in zip-top plastic freezer bag
- Pack all menu items and paper products for travel

Just before serving:

- Spread the blanket and relax

Chunky Sour Cream Dip

makes 3 cups   hands-on time: 8 min.   total time: 8 min.

Chopped tomato and hot sauce perk up this simple Ranch dip.

1   (8-oz.) container sour cream
1   (8-oz.) container garden vegetable dip
1   (1-oz.) packet Ranch dressing mix
¾   cup finely chopped tomato

¼   tsp. hot sauce
Corn chips
Carrot sticks

1. Combine first 3 ingredients, stirring well. Stir in tomato and hot sauce. Cover and chill until ready to serve. Serve dip with corn chips and carrot sticks.
Note: We tested with Rondelé Garden Vegetable Dip.

Basil Egg Salad on Sourdough

makes 8 servings   hands-on time: 20 min.   total time: 20 min.

If traveling farther than your backyard, wrap these gourmet sandwiches in parchment paper, place in zip-top plastic bags, and nestle them around a freezer pack in your cooler until you reach your prime picnic destination.

12 medium-size hard-cooked eggs, chopped
4   bacon slices, cooked and crumbled
⅔   cup mayonnaise
½   cup chopped fresh basil
2   Tbsp. minced shallot
2   tsp. white wine vinegar
¼   tsp. salt

¼   tsp. freshly cracked pepper
½   cup mayonnaise
16 sourdough bread slices
½   cup firmly packed baby spinach
¼   cup firmly packed fresh basil leaves
Parchment paper (optional)

1. Combine first 8 ingredients in a bowl; stir well. Cover and chill until ready to assemble.
2. Spread ½ cup mayonnaise on 1 side of bread slices. Spread egg salad mixture on 8 bread slices; top with spinach and basil leaves. Top with remaining 8 bread slices, mayonnaise sides down. Cut each sandwich in half, and wrap in parchment paper, if desired.
Note: We tested with Eggland's Best Hard-Cooked Peeled Eggs and Pepperidge Farm Sourdough Bread.

"Ice packs are a must when the mercury is high. Metal containers stay cold longer, and galvanized pails can be turned into individual ice buckets for keeping beverages chilled."

Black-eyed Pea and Veggie Salad

makes 8 servings   hands-on time: 12 min.   total time: 12 min.

This simple pea salad makes ideal picnic fare. The longer it sits, the better it tastes.

2   (15.8-oz.) cans black-eyed peas, drained and rinsed
1   red bell pepper, finely chopped
1   jalapeño pepper, seeded and minced
3   Tbsp. balsamic vinegar
2   Tbsp. olive oil

1   Tbsp. honey
½   cup diced ham
1   cup refrigerated prechopped celery, green bell pepper, and onion

1. Combine first 6 ingredients in a bowl, stirring well.
2. Sauté ham in a medium skillet over medium-high heat 1 to 2 minutes or until browned. Add celery mixture; sauté 1 minute. Add sautéed mixture to pea salad. Serve at room temperature, or cover and chill until ready to serve.

PB & Chocolate Pan Cookie

makes about 24 pieces   hands-on time: 10 min.   total time: **30 min.**

Leave the mixer in the cabinet—you can mix up this dough with a spoon.

¾ cup chunky peanut butter
2 large eggs
1 tsp. vanilla extract

1 cup firmly packed light brown sugar
2 cups all-purpose baking mix
1 (12-oz.) package dark chocolate morsels, divided

1. Preheat oven to 325°. Stir together peanut butter, eggs, and vanilla in a large bowl.
2. Stir in brown sugar until combined. Add baking mix and ¾ cup dark chocolate morsels, stirring just until dry ingredients are moistened. Spread mixture in a lightly greased 15- x 10-inch jelly-roll pan.
3. Bake at 325° for 20 minutes or until golden brown. Remove from oven, and sprinkle with remaining 1¼ cups dark chocolate morsels; let stand until chocolate melts. Spread melted chocolate over top of cookie. Cut into triangles.
Note: We tested with Bisquick All-Purpose Baking Mix and Hershey's Special Dark Chips.

Strawberry Cheesecake Trifle

Mile-High Marshmallow-Chocolate Slabs

Caramel Cake Ba

dessert party

menu

---

serves 12

Ultimate Alexander

Rosemary-Lemon Cornmeal Cakes

Strawberry Cheesecake Trifle

Caramel Cake Balls

Mile-High Marshmallow-Chocolate Slabs

Try something new, and invite friends over for an after-dinner coffee drink and a sweet sampling of indulgent treats. Arrange the goodies on dishes of varying heights for interest. Create recipe labels freehand or with the computer to set out with your dessert plates.

hostess
hit list:

The perfect dessert assortment has something for everyone—a nibble of chocolate, a burst of citrus, a bit of berry, and dare we say, a delectable morsel that is over the top. Lean on store-bought treats to make it happen.

The day before:
- Bake cornmeal cakes
- Make trifle; cover and chill
- Prepare cake balls and scoop; cover
- Prepare chocolate slabs; cover and freeze
- Gather all serving pieces, and set table

30 minutes before:
- Make crème fraîche
- Dip cake balls, and garnish
- Remove chocolate slab from freezer, and let thaw

15 minutes before:
- Slice chocolate slab
- Prepare garnishes for the Ultimate Alexander

Just before serving:
- Prepare the Ultimate Alexander
- Assemble cornmeal cakes

Ultimate Alexander

Ultimate Alexander

makes 5 cups   hands-on time: 5 min.   total time: 5 min.

One recipe fills the blender and will serve five to six people. Prepare 2 recipes to serve a party of 12.

¼ cup cold brewed coffee
2 (14-oz.) containers coffee ice cream
½ cup brandy

½ cup chocolate syrup
Garnishes: sweetened whipped cream, chocolate curls,
        chocolate fudge cream-filled rolled wafer cookies

1. Process cold brewed coffee, ice cream, brandy, and chocolate syrup in a blender until smooth, stopping to scrape down sides. Pour mixture into glasses, and garnish, if desired. Serve immediately.
Note: We tested with Häagen-Dazs Coffee ice cream and Pepperidge Farm Chocolate Fudge Pirouette Rolled Wafers.

Rosemary-Lemon Cornmeal Cakes

makes 12 servings   hands-on time: 10 min.   total time: 28 min.

If you collect cast-iron skillets, pull out a few small pans and bake these rustic cornmeal cakes in no time. Otherwise, pour the batter into a large cast-iron skillet, and bake a little longer.

Shortening
1¼ cups all-purpose flour
1 cup granulated sugar
½ cup plain yellow cornmeal
1 Tbsp. chopped fresh rosemary
½ tsp. baking soda
¼ tsp. salt
⅔ cup buttermilk

¼ cup butter, melted
2 large eggs
2 tsp. lemon zest
½ cup crème fraîche
1 Tbsp. turbinado sugar
1 pt. fresh blueberries
Garnish: fresh rosemary

1. Preheat oven to 350°. Coat 3 (6-inch) cast-iron skillets with shortening. Combine flour and next 5 ingredients; stir well. Combine buttermilk and next 3 ingredients; add to flour mixture, stirring until dry ingredients are moistened. Pour batter into prepared skillets.
2. Bake at 350° for 18 to 19 minutes or until a wooden pick inserted in center comes out clean. Cool in skillets on a wire rack.
3. Meanwhile, stir together crème fraîche and turbinado sugar; cover and chill until ready to serve.
4. Remove cakes from skillets, and cut into wedges. Top each serving with a small dollop of crème fraîche mixture and berries. Garnish, if desired.

Strawberry Cheesecake Trifle

makes 10 to 12 servings   hands-on time: 15 min.   **total time: 15 min.**

Frozen cheesecake bites star in this simple dessert.

1 (15-oz.) store-bought angel food cake
2 (7-oz.) containers frozen strawberry cheesecake bites
3 (4-oz.) containers refrigerated vanilla pudding

1 (8-oz.) container sour cream
2 cups thawed extra-creamy whipped topping
½ cup sliced fresh strawberries

1. Cut cake into 1-inch slices. Cut slices into 1-inch cubes to yield 6 cups. Reserve remaining cake for another use.

2. Place half of cake cubes in a 3-qt. trifle bowl. Top with half of cheesecake bites. Stir together pudding and sour cream until blended. Spoon half of pudding mixture over cheesecake bites. Repeat layers once. Top with whipped topping and strawberries. Cover and chill until ready to serve.

Note: We tested with Sara Lee Cheesecake Bites and Swiss Miss Creamy Pudding.

Caramel Cake Balls

makes 28 servings   hands-on time: 30 min.   total time: 30 min.

You can't beat the convenience of using a store-bought layer cake to make these nifty little cake balls. We sprinkled some with orange zest and left some plain to give guests a choice.

½ (48-oz.) store-bought caramel cake
Wax paper
1 (4-oz.) white chocolate baking bar, chopped

1 tsp. shortening
½ tsp. orange zest, divided
28 paper baking cups

1. Crumble cake into a bowl. Beat at medium speed with an electric mixer just until blended (about 30 seconds). Scoop cake mixture into 28 (1-inch) balls using a cookie scoop or melon baller, and place on a wax paper-lined jelly-roll pan.

2. Melt white chocolate, shortening, and ¼ tsp. orange zest in a small microwave-safe glass bowl at MEDIUM (50%) power 1½ minutes; stir until smooth. Quickly dip top of each cake ball into chocolate mixture. Place cake balls, dipped sides up, in paper baking cups. Sprinkle half of cake balls with remaining ¼ tsp. orange zest.

Note: We tested with a seven-layer caramel cake from Dean's Cake House. These cakes can be found at grocery stores and some gas stations across the South, or call (334) 222-0459, or you can use any bakery caramel cake.

Mile-High Marshmallow-Chocolate Slabs

makes 30 servings   hands-on time: 10 min.   total time: 30 min.

If you have time, freeze longer for a cleaner slice, or toast the nuts for this wickedly rich chocolate dessert.

1 (12-oz.) package semisweet chocolate morsels
1½ cups milk chocolate morsels
½ cup creamy peanut butter
4 cups miniature marshmallows

1 cup coarsely chopped pecans
¾ cup chopped natural almonds
1 (7-oz.) package dark chocolate-coated pretzels, coarsely crushed (2 cups)

1. Line an 11- x 7-inch baking dish with lightly-greased aluminum foil, allowing 2 to 3 inches to extend over sides.

2. Combine first 3 ingredients in a large microwave-safe glass bowl. Microwave, uncovered, at MEDIUM-HIGH (70%) power 2 to 2½ minutes; stir until smooth. Stir in marshmallows, nuts, and pretzels.

3. Spread chocolate mixture into prepared pan. Cover loosely, and freeze 20 minutes or until firm enough to slice. Invert uncut chocolate onto a cutting board; remove foil. Invert again, and cut crosswise into 1-inch-thick sticks. Cut each stick into 2¼-inch-long slabs. Store in an airtight container in refrigerator up to 5 days.

Note: We tested with Snyder's pretzels.

simple
celebrations

The recipe for any great party requires friends, food, and fun. Entertaining the *Half-Hour Hostess* way is all about focusing on what's deliciously easy to pull off so that you can turn your focus to what the party is all about. Here you'll find inspiration for good times that require minimal effort.

valentine's day
dinner

menu

serves 4

tray of assorted cheeses, French bread slices, and grapes

Pan-Seared Flat-Iron Steak

Creamed Turnip Greens

Easy Garlic Rolls

Ultimate Chocolate Pudding

Toss the pressure of what to do for Valentine's Day right out the window with this easy menu for four. Invite another couple to join you, or plan to enjoy the meal twice. Serve this elegant spread on a table simply dressed with a pretty cloth, crisp white china, and a few flowers in bud vases.

hostess
hit list:

Unwrap an assortment of cheeses—aged Cheddar, Parmigiano, Camembert, and Gorgonzola are a good mix—and let them come to room temperature while you prepare the meal.

The day before:

- Prepare pudding; cover and chill
- Thaw turnip greens in refrigerator
- Set the table
- Wash grapes; chill
- Arrange flowers

30 minutes before:

- Prepare flat-iron steak
- Prepare turnip greens

15 minutes before:

- Prepare garlic rolls
- Open wine

Just before serving:

- Garnish pudding, and place cookies on dessert plates
- Pour wine

Pan-Seared Flat-Iron Steak

makes 4 servings   hands-on time: 13 min.   total time: 18 min.

The trick to a great crust on this flat-iron steak is to use a very hot skillet; a large cast-iron or heavy stainless steel skillet works best. Have your hood fan on high—there will be some smoke. If you can't find flat-iron steak in your local market, a top blade chuck or sirloin steak will work just fine.

1   (1-lb.) flat-iron steak
2   tsp. Montreal steak seasoning

¼   tsp. kosher salt
1   Tbsp. vegetable oil

1. Rub steak with steak seasoning and salt.

2. Cook steak in hot oil in a large skillet over medium-high heat 4 to 5 minutes on each side or to desired degree of doneness. Let stand 5 minutes. Cut diagonally across the grain into thin strips.

Note: We tested with McCormick Grill Mates Montreal Steak Seasoning.

Creamed Turnip Greens

makes 4 servings   hands-on time: 25 min.   total time: 25 min.

You'll love this Southern spin on a steakhouse favorite.

1   Tbsp. butter
½   sweet onion, chopped
2   garlic cloves, minced
1   (16-oz.) package frozen turnip greens, thawed
½   cup chicken broth

½   tsp. dried crushed red pepper (optional)
2   Tbsp. all-purpose flour
1   cup milk
5   oz. cream cheese, cut into pieces
Salt to taste

1. Melt butter in a large nonstick skillet over medium-high heat. Stir in onion and garlic, and sauté 3 minutes or until tender. Stir in turnip greens, chicken broth, and, if desired, red pepper; cook 4 to 5 minutes or until liquid evaporates.

2. Sprinkle turnip green mixture with flour, and sauté 2 minutes. Gradually stir in milk, and cook, stirring occasionally, 3 minutes. Add cream cheese, stirring until melted. Season with salt to taste.

> **"**Leftovers make terrific cheesesteak sandwiches. Top hoagie rolls with sautéed onions, peppers, sliced beef, and provolone, and then toast under the broiler until cheese melts.**"**

Easy Garlic Rolls

makes 4 to 6 servings   hands-on time: 8 min.   total time: 15 min.

4   French bread rolls

½   cup butter, softened

2   garlic cloves, minced

¼ to ½ tsp. dried Italian seasoning

1. Preheat oven to 400°. Cut rolls in half horizontally. Stir together softened butter, garlic, and Italian seasoning; spread butter mixture on cut sides of bread. Place bread, cut sides up, on a lightly greased baking sheet. Bake 7 to 8 minutes or until lightly toasted.

Ultimate Chocolate Pudding

makes 4 servings   hands-on time: 20 min.   total time: 30 min.

1 ¼ cups sugar

½   cup Dutch process cocoa

¼   cup cornstarch

½   tsp. salt

2½ cups milk

⅓   cup unsalted butter, cut up

2   tsp. vanilla extract

Unsweetened whipped cream

Chocolate-filled vanilla wafer sandwich cookies

1. Whisk together first 4 ingredients in a medium saucepan. Gradually whisk in milk. Cook over medium heat, stirring constantly, until pudding boils and is thickened (about 8 to 10 minutes). Reduce heat to medium-low, and cook 2 more minutes. Remove from heat; add butter and vanilla, stirring gently until butter melts. Place heavy-duty plastic wrap directly on warm pudding (to prevent a film from forming); cool 10 minutes.
2. Serve warm, or cover with plastic wrap, and chill until ready to serve (up to 24 hours). Top with whipped cream, and stir gently to blend. Serve with cookies.
Note: We tested with Pepperidge Farm Milano cookies.

"Chocolate desserts are always crowd-pleasers, so when in doubt, go dark and decadent!"

mardi gras party

menu

---

serves 8

Hurricane Punch

Easy Mini Muffulettas

Easy Chicken Gumbo

King Cake Cupcakes

If there is one place known for its parties, it's New Orleans. So take a cue from the Crescent City, and let the good times roll from start to finish with festive fare that tastes like it's straight from the French Quarter.

hostess
hit list:

Turn on some zydeco, bluegrass, or jazz and pass the Hurricane Punch. Let folks mingle before directing them to the food table.

The day before:

- Make punch; cover and chill
- Prepare gumbo, and cool completely; cover and chill
- Frost cupcakes, and sprinkle with sugars

🕐 30 minutes before:

- Assemble Easy Mini Muffulettas
- Remove gumbo from refrigerator, and reheat on stovetop
- Prepare rice for gumbo

🕐 15 minutes before:

- Bake muffulettas
- Place ice in glasses for punch
- Slice French bread for gumbo

🕐 Just before serving:

- Pour punch in glasses
- Ladle gumbo into bowls
- Place muffulettas on platter

Hurricane Punch

makes 8¼ cups   hands-on time: 10 min.   total time: 10 min.

½ (64-oz.) bottle red fruit punch
½ (12-oz.) can frozen limeade concentrate, thawed
1 (6-oz.) can frozen orange juice concentrate, thawed

1⅔ cups light rum
1⅔ cups dark rum

1. Stir together all ingredients. Serve over ice.

Easy Mini Muffulettas

makes 12 servings   hands-on time: 15 min.   total time: 29 min.

The muffuletta was named after the Sicilian flat, round loaf on which it was first served at New Orleans' City Grocery in the early 1900s.

2 (16-oz.) jars Italian olive salad
12 small deli rolls, cut in half
12 thin Swiss cheese slices

12 thin deli ham slices
12 thin provolone cheese slices
12 Genoa salami slices

1. Preheat oven to 350°. Spread 1 Tbsp. olive salad over each cut side of roll bottoms. Top each with 1 Swiss cheese slice, 1 ham slice, 1 Tbsp. olive salad, 1 provolone cheese slice, 1 salami slice, and 1 Tbsp. olive salad. Cover with roll tops, and wrap sandwiches together in a large piece of aluminum foil. Place on a baking sheet.
2. Bake at 350° for 14 to 16 minutes or until cheeses are melted.
Note: We tested with Boscoli Family Italian Olive Salad.

hip tip Vases and bowls overflowing with **metallic beads** in Mardi Gras purple, gold, and green are inexpensive decorations that guests can take home as favors.

Easy Chicken Gumbo

makes 6 servings   hands-on time: 18 min.   total time: 28 min.

½ cup peanut oil
½ cup all-purpose flour
1 (10-oz.) package frozen diced onion, red and green bell peppers, and celery
1½ to 3 tsp. Cajun seasoning
2 tsp. minced garlic

3 (14-oz.) cans chicken broth
½ lb. andouille sausage, cut in ¼-inch-thick slices
4 cups chopped cooked chicken
Hot cooked rice
1 (16-oz.) French bread loaf, sliced

1. Heat oil in a large Dutch oven over medium-high heat; gradually whisk in flour, and cook, whisking constantly, 5 minutes or until flour is chocolate-colored. (Do not burn mixture.)
2. Reduce heat to medium. Stir in diced onion mixture and next 2 ingredients, and cook, stirring constantly, 3 minutes. Gradually stir in chicken broth and sausage. Increase heat to medium-high, and bring to a boil. Reduce heat to low, and simmer, stirring occasionally, 10 to 20 minutes.
3. Stir chicken into gumbo; cook, stirring occasionally, 5 minutes. Serve with hot cooked rice and bread.

“Be sure to use peanut oil when making our 5-minute roux. It can withstand higher heat than vegetable oil without burning.**”**

King Cake Cupcakes

makes 12 servings   hands-on time: 14 min.   total time: 30 min.

These shortcut sweets make enjoying Mardi Gras easy, as each little cake can be eaten out of hand. The trademark decorations of these treats—sugars in the royal colors of purple (justice), green (faith), and gold (power)—honor the three kings who visted the Christ child on Epiphany, the 12th day after Christmas. Also known as King's Day, it marks the start of merrymaking that continues until the grand finale on Fat Tuesday, the day before Ash Wednesday. Good luck goes to the one who picks the cupcake with a tiny plastic baby tucked inside.

½   (8-oz.) package cream cheese, softened
¼   cup butter, softened
1½ cups powdered sugar
¼   tsp. vanilla extract

2   to 3 Tbsp. half-and-half
12 unfrosted, store-bought cupcakes
Green-, purple-, and gold-tinted sparkling sugar

1. Beat cream cheese and butter at medium speed with an electric mixer until creamy. Gradually add sugar, beating until blended. Stir in vanilla and 2 Tbsp half-and-half. Add remaining half-and-half, 1 tsp. at a time, until desired consistency. Spread frosting over cupcakes. Sprinkle with colored sugars, alternating colors and forming bands.

Note: If desired, insert a heatproof plastic baby doll token into one cupcake before frosting.

quick finds King cake babies can be ordered from www.mardigrasoutlet.com, and retail for about $1.49 per package of 36. Look for them at **cake supply** stores, too.

st. patrick's day

menu

Green Beer

Three-Bite Reubens

Pub Slaw with Beets

Quick Irish Cream Fudge

Go green the Irish way, surrounded by friends. Put on some Celtic tunes, pass around frosty mugs of green beer, and say a few words in honor of the Patron Saint of Ireland; then dig in to a traditional Irish fare of hearty reubens and slaw with earthy beets. End it with a fudgy dessert spiked with Irish cream.

hostess
hit list:

Consider yourself extra-lucky this St. Patrick's day, because the decor for this gathering has an obvious palette. Go green from flowers to table and even the drink!

The day before:
- Make slaw dressing
- Make fudge; cover and chill

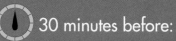 ### 30 minutes before:
- Make reubens
- Assemble slaw

15 minutes before:
- Slice fudge, and place on serving piece

Just before serving:
- Make Green Beer

Green Beer

makes 15 cups   hands-on time: 5 min.   total time: 5 min.

There's no stirring needed for this festive beverage. Two drops is the right amount to get a nice olive green color. Three drops will result in more of a kelly green shade, as shown in the photo.

Green liquid food coloring
10 bottles or cans of favorite beer

1. Place 3 drops of green liquid food coloring in bottom of 10 beer mugs or glasses. Add beer.

Three-Bite Reubens

makes 10 to 12 servings   hands-on time: 18 min.   total time: 18 min.

Corned beef is traditional to St. Patty's Day. Here, it is featured in Reuben finger sandwiches. Spear them with green-tassled party picks for luck.

⅓   cup Russian dressing
12 (1-oz.) rye bread slices
12 (0.67-oz.) Swiss cheese slices
1   cup refrigerated sauerkraut, drained

¾   lb. shaved deli corned beef
⅓   cup mayonnaise
½   cup butter, softened

1. Spread dressing on 1 side of 6 bread slices. Top with 1 cheese slice, sauerkraut, corned beef, and another cheese slice.
2. Spread mayonnaise on 1 side of remaining 6 bread slices, and place, mayonnaise sides down, on top of cheese.
3. Spread both sides of sandwiches with butter.
4. Heat a large nonstick skillet or griddle over medium heat. Cook sandwiches, in batches, 2 minutes on each side or until bread is golden and cheese melts. Cut each sandwich crosswise into 4 pieces.

hip tip Feel free to substitute **deli smoked turkey** for corned beef.

> **"**Look for floral accents in shades of green—shamrocks, belles of Ireland, or mums for looks and luck.**"**

Pub Slaw with Beets

makes 10 servings   hands-on time: 15 min.   total time: 15 min.

Capers and pickled beets balance salty and sour tastes in this favorite slaw with onions and chopped eggs.

½ cup mayonnaise
¼ cup dill pickle relish
2 Tbsp. drained capers
1 Tbsp. malt vinegar
1 Tbsp. stone-ground mustard
1 tsp. chopped fresh tarragon

½ tsp. freshly ground pepper
1 (10-oz.) package finely shredded cabbage
½ cup thinly sliced red onion
2 hard-cooked eggs, peeled and chopped
1¼ cup canned sliced pickled beets, cut into thin strips

1. Stir together first 7 ingredients in a large bowl. Add cabbage, onion, and eggs; toss well. Add beets; toss gently just until combined.

Quick Irish Cream Fudge

Makes 1 lb., 6 oz.   hands-on time: 5 min.   total time: 30 min.

Have your liqueur, and eat it too, in fudge that satisfies your sweet tooth with each creamy bite.

½ cup butter, melted
1 (16-oz.) package powdered sugar
¼ cup Dutch process cocoa

1 tsp. vanilla extract
¼ cup Irish cream liqueur

1. Line bottom and sides of an 8-inch square pan with aluminum foil, allowing 2 to 3 inches to extend over sides.
2. Place all ingredients in a large bowl; beat at medium speed with a electric mixer until smooth. Press mixture into prepared pan. Cover and chill 25 minutes or until firm. Lift fudge from pan, using foil sides as handles. Cut into 1-inch squares.

casual easter
brunch

menu

serves 8

Ham Steaks with Orange-Bourbon-Pecan Sauce

Asparagus-and-Mushroom Bread Puddings

fresh cut fruit

Easter Egg Thumbprints

White Chocolate Easter Candy Bark

pink lemonade

Celebrate springtime with this flavorful and seasonal menu.
Look for tips sprinkled throughout that will help you have this
meal prepared in a snap, allowing you more time for a fun-filled
afternoon Easter egg hunt.

hostess
hit list:

This easy meal comes together quickly, and the desserts can be made in advance. Or better yet, set up a cookie-decorating station outside for the kids the day of the party, if the weather permits.

The day before:

- Bake Easter thumbprint cookies; cover
- Prepare candy bark; cover
- Prepare fruit; cover and chill

30 minutes before:

- Prepare and bake bread puddings

15 minutes before:

- Prepare ham steaks and sauce

Just before serving:

- Place cookies and candy on serving platters
- Plate food

Ham Steaks with Orange-Bourbon-Pecan Sauce

makes 8 servings   hands-on time: 18 min.   total time: 18 min.

Sweet-tart marmalade complements the smokiness of the ham.

2   Tbsp. butter
2   (1½-lb.) lean ham steaks
1   tsp. freshly ground pepper

½   cup chopped pecans
½   cup orange marmalade
2   Tbsp. bourbon or orange juice

1. Melt 1 Tbsp. butter in a 12-inch cast-iron skillet over medium-high heat. Sprinkle ham steaks with pepper. Cook 1 ham steak in melted butter 3 minutes on each side or until golden. Transfer to a serving platter. Repeat procedure with remaining 1 Tbsp. butter and ham steak. Cover and keep warm.

2. Cook pecans in a medium-size nonstick skillet over medium-low heat, stirring often, 5 minutes or until toasted and fragrant. Remove skillet from heat; add marmalade and bourbon, and return to heat. Cook, stirring constantly, 1 minute or until marmalade melts. Serve sauce with ham steaks.

Asparagus-and-Mushroom Bread Puddings

makes 8 servings   hands-on time: 15 min.   total time: 30 min.

Divide and conquer time by baking in individual dishes. These personal casseroles bake in less than half the time of a large dish.

1   (1-lb.) bunch thin fresh asparagus
Vegetable cooking spray
1   (8-oz.) package sliced fresh mushrooms
5   large eggs
12 oz. Swiss cheese, shredded
2½ cups milk

1   Tbsp. chopped fresh chives
2   tsp. chopped fresh dill
1   tsp. salt
½   tsp. freshly ground pepper
1   (12-oz.) French bread loaf, cut into 1-inch cubes

1. Preheat oven to 375°. Snap off and discard tough ends of asparagus. Cut asparagus into 1-inch pieces. Heat a large nonstick skillet over medium-high heat. Coat pan with cooking spray. Add asparagus and mushrooms; sauté 5 minutes or just until asparagus is tender.

2. Whisk eggs in a large bowl; whisk in half of cheese and next 5 ingredients. Add asparagus mixture and bread cubes, stirring to coat. Spoon bread mixture into 8 lightly greased (10-oz.) custard cups or ramekins. Sprinkle with remaining half of cheese. Place cups on a large baking sheet.

3. Bake at 375° for 15 minutes or until set and lightly browned.

Note: We used pencil-thin asparagus for faster cooking.

Easter Egg Thumbprints

makes 12 servings   **hands-on time: 12 min.**   **total time: 30 min.,** not including cooling

If you can't find malted milk eggs in Easter colors, look for them online or substitute jelly beans, as we did here.

1 (16-oz.) package refrigerated sugar cookie dough   ½ cup ready-to-spread cream cheese frosting
⅓ cup all-purpose flour   24 jelly beans and Jordan almonds
Parchment paper

1. Preheat oven to 350°. Knead together dough and flour in a large bowl until blended. Shape dough mixture into 24 (1-inch) balls, and place ½ inch apart on a parchment paper-lined baking sheet. Press thumb into each ball, forming an indentation.
2. Bake at 350° for 18 minutes or until edges are lightly browned. Transfer to wire racks, and cool completely (about 20 minutes).
3. Spoon frosting into a zip-top plastic freezer bag. Snip off 1 corner of bag to make a small hole. Pipe about 1 tsp. frosting into each cookie indentation; top with jelly beans and Jordan almonds.
Note: We tested with Pillsbury sugar cookie dough and Betty Crocker frosting.

White Chocolate Easter Candy Bark

makes 2¼ lb.   hands-on time: 12 min.   total time: 12 min., not including standing

It takes about 30 minutes for the bark candy to get firm enough so you'll want to make it ahead. We used a generic brand of mint-flavored candy eggs from the supermarket, but substitute any variety of candy.

Parchment paper   2   cups small pastel-colored candy eggs
2   (12-oz.) packages white chocolate candy coating

1. Line 2 jelly-roll pans with parchment paper.
2. Melt chocolate coating according to package directions. Pour chocolate into prepared pans, and spread in an even layer. Sprinkle candy eggs over chocolate. Let stand until coating is firm (about 30 minutes). Invert pans, and remove; discard parchment. Break candy into large pieces.

"Egg cups lend charm to the table. Cupcake liners, Easter grass, and baby's breath become 'nests' for flowers, candy, and Easter eggs personalized as placeholders."

baby shower

menu

serves 12 to 18

Curried Shrimp Tarts

Ham-and-Cheese Skewers

Cucumber-Dill Soup

Cheesecake Petits Fours

lemonade

Special times deserve special attention. Shower an expecting
new mom-to-be with gifts and well-wishes she'll hold dear forever.
Decorate with blue or pink if you're in the know, or keep things
neutral with yellow, green, or all white to play it safe. This menu
of tasty little morsels is perfectly fitting for the occasion.

hostess
hit list:

The beauty of this menu is that it's all about planning and assembly, equaling one relaxed hostess.

The day before:

- Make curried shrimp mixture; cover and chill
- Prepare soup; cover and chill
- Prepare Cheesecake Petits Fours; decorate and chill

30 minutes before:

- Make and assemble skewers; cover with damp paper towels until ready to serve

15 minutes before:

- Remove soup from fridge; stir; pour into shot glasses
- Spoon shrimp mixture into phyllo shells

Just before serving:

- Garnish soup
- Top shrimp tarts with garnishes
- Pour lemonade into glasses

Curried Shrimp Tarts

makes 12 to 18 servings   hands-on time: 25 min.   total time: 25 min.

Zap cream cheese in the microwave for 5 to 10 seconds to soften quickly. Purchase 1½ lb. unpeeled shrimp to get a 3-cup yield.

3   cups chopped cooked shrimp
1½ (8-oz.) packages cream cheese, softened
5   Tbsp. chopped green onions
2   Tbsp. fresh lime juice
1¼ tsp. curry powder
½   tsp. ground red pepper

3   (1.9-oz.) packages frozen mini-phyllo pastry shells, thawed
½   cup jarred mango chutney
Toppings: chopped fresh chives, toasted sweetened flaked coconut

1. Stir together first 6 ingredients. Spoon mixture into pastry shells. Spoon ½ tsp. mango chutney over each tart; sprinkle with desired toppings.

Ham-and-Cheese Skewers

makes 12 to 18 servings   hands-on time: 25 min.   total time: 25 min.

Assemble up to one hour ahead, cover with damp paper towels, and chill. Serve with coarse-grain mustard for dipping.

½   lb. smoked Virginia deli ham slices (¾-inch-thick)
1   (5-oz.) blue cheese wedge
1   large Gala apple, cut into bite-size pieces

1   bunch fresh watercress
30 (4-inch) wooden or metal skewers

1. Cut ham into ¾-inch cubes. Carefully break cheese into 30 small pieces. Cut apple slices into thirds.
2. Thread apple, watercress leaves, cheese, and ham onto skewers. Stand skewers upright, ham ends down, on a serving plate.

hip tip Place a pretty **journal** in your entryway for your guests to write well-wishes to the honoree.

Cucumber-Dill Soup

makes 4 cups   hands-on time: 10 min.   total time: 10 min.

Shot glasses are a fun way to serve this tasty soup. One recipe yields about 32 (1-oz.) portions, so pick up additional shot glasses, if necessary. Expect each guest to indulge in two.

2   cucumbers, peeled, seeded, and coarsely chopped
1   green onion, coarsely chopped
1   Tbsp. lemon juice
1   (16-oz.) container sour cream
1   cup half-and-half

1   Tbsp. minced fresh dill
1   tsp. salt
¼   tsp. pepper
⅛   tsp. hot sauce
Garnish: fresh dill sprigs

1. Process first 3 ingredients in a blender or food processor until smooth, stopping to scrape down sides. Pour into a large bowl; stir in sour cream and next 5 ingredients. Cover and chill until ready to serve (up to 24 hours.) Garnish, if desired.

"Pacifiers make adorable napkin rings, and baby bottles stand in as bud vases. Arrange gifts on a tiered stand, and they'll become your centerpiece."

Cheesecake Petits Fours

makes about 2½ dozen   hands-on time: 27 min.   total time: 27 min.

Jump-start these rich little cakes by using delectable store-bought cheesecake that you decorate and personalize.

½   cup butter, softened
1   tsp. vanilla extract
⅛   tsp. salt
1   (16-oz.) package powdered sugar

3 to 5 Tbsp. milk
Red, yellow, and green food coloring paste
2   (30-oz.) frozen New York-style cheesecakes, thawed
2   Tbsp. cornstarch

1. Beat first 3 ingredients at medium speed with an electric mixer until creamy. Gradually add powdered sugar alternately with 3 Tbsp. milk, 1 Tbsp. at a time, beating at low speed until blended and smooth after each addition. Beat in up to 2 Tbsp. additional for desired consistency.
2. Divide frosting into fourths; place in small bowls. Tint 3 bowls each with a different color of food coloring paste, and stir until blended. Insert metal tip no. 7 (small round tip) into a large decorating bag; fill with white frosting.
3. Trim edges of each cheesecake to form a square; cut each into 16 squares (about 1¼ inches), and place on a serving tray.
4. Insert metal tip no. 12 (large round tip) into a large decorating bag; fill with pink frosting. Pipe baby booties or desired decorations onto one-third of petits fours. Dip fingertip repeatedly in cornstarch, and make indentations into tops of booties. Repeat procedure with yellow and green frostings and cornstarch, using same metal tip and piping yellow and green booties on remaining cheesecakes. Pipe bows onto booties using white frosting. Cover loosely, and chill until ready to serve.
Note: We tested with Sara Lee Cheesecakes.

fast flourish If piping frosting isn't your thing, embellish the petits fours with candies, berries, or a drizzle of chocolate or caramel syrup.

mother's day
luncheon

menu

serves 6

Sparkling Wine Fruit Refresher

Fresh Basil Pasta Salad

Sherried Chicken-and-Grape Salad

fresh fruit

Free-form Strawberry Cheesecake

Show your mother she raised you right by doting on her during her special day. For a sophisticated look stick to a simple palette of two or three colors, and repeat them over and over again. Don't be afraid to combine bone china with plastic utensils and paper napkins from the party store. It's a simple way to keep the tone of the party light.

hostess
hit list:

Enjoy drinks on the porch or patio, and catch up for a bit before you take your leave to serve the food. Except for the dessert, it all goes straight from the fridge to the plate.

The day before:

- Chill lemon-lime soft drink and Champagne
- Cook pasta for salad; cover and chill
- Make dressing for pasta salad; cover and chill
- Toast pine nuts for pasta salad
- Make chicken salad; cover and chill
- Prepare fruit; cover and chill

30 minutes before:

- Assemble pasta salad and chill until ready to serve

15 minutes before:

- Assemble cheesecakes

Just before serving:

- Prepare beverages
- Garnish cheesecakes

Sparkling Wine Fruit Refresher

makes 6 servings   hands-on time: 10 min.   total time: 10 min.

Keep this recipe handy for your next brunch. It's a great alternative to mimosas. Another idea: Add a diced kiwifruit to your favorite mixed berries in this versatile, light cocktail.

1   cup lemon-lime soft drink, chilled
1   cup assorted berries
1   (6-oz.) can frozen limeade concentrate, thawed

¼   cup loosely packed fresh mint or basil leaves, torn
1   (750-milliliter) bottle sparkling white wine or Champagne, chilled

1. Combine first 4 ingredients in a large pitcher. Gently stir in sparkling wine. Serve immediately.

Sparkling Fruit Refresher: Substitute 3 (12-oz.) cans orange-flavored sparkling water, chilled, for sparkling white wine. Proceed with recipe as directed.

Fresh Basil Pasta Salad

makes 8 servings   hands-on time: 20 min.   total time: 20 min.

1   (16-oz.) package small shell pasta
½   cup pine nuts
⅓   cup red wine vinegar
1   Tbsp. sugar
1   tsp. seasoned pepper
1   tsp. Dijon mustard

½   tsp. salt
1   garlic clove, pressed
¾   cup olive oil
1   cup chopped fresh basil
1   (3-oz.) package shredded Parmesan cheese

1. Prepare pasta according to package directions.

2. Meanwhile, heat pine nuts in a skillet over medium-high heat, stirring often, 5 minutes or until toasted and fragrant.

3. Whisk together vinegar and next 5 ingredients. Add oil in a slow, steady stream, whisking constantly until smooth. Add vinaigrette to pasta. Add basil, cheese, and pine nuts; toss to combine. Cover and chill until ready to serve.

"I like to pull out all the stops for mom. So dress the table, garnish the food, and show her how much you care."

Sherried Chicken-and-Grape Salad

makes 6 to 8 servings   hands-on time: 10 min.   total time: 27 min.

Toasted walnuts can be substituted for the almonds. Cool completely before using.

1   cup slivered almonds
6   cups chopped cooked chicken
3   cups halved seedless green or red grapes
2   celery ribs, diced
3   green onions, minced
¾   cup mayonnaise

¼   cup sour cream
2   Tbsp. sherry
½   tsp. seasoned salt
½   tsp. seasoned pepper
Mixed spring greens (optional)

1. Preheat oven to 350°. Bake almonds in a single layer in a shallow pan 7 to 9 minutes or until toasted and fragrant, stirring halfway through. Let cool 10 minutes.

2. Stir together almonds, chicken, and next 8 ingredients. Cover and chill until ready to serve (up to 24 hours). Serve chicken salad over mixed spring greens, if desired.

fast flourish Turn a simple **white mug** into a stunner by filling it with a single-variety bouquet or a mix of a similar hue.

Free-form Strawberry Cheesecake

makes 6 servings   hands-on time: 20 min.   total time: 20 min.

Powdered sugar saves time and dissolves instantly when stirred into berries for an almost effortless dessert.

2   cups fresh strawberries, sliced

4   Tbsp. powdered sugar, divided

1½ cups ready-to-eat cheesecake filling

1   tsp. lime zest

1   Tbsp. lime juice

6   crisp gourmet cookies, crumbled

Garnishes: crisp gourmet cookies, lime slices

1. Stir together strawberries and 2 Tbsp. powdered sugar.

2. Stir together cheesecake filling, lime zest, lime juice, and remaining 2 Tbsp. powdered sugar.

3. Spoon cheesecake mixture into 6 (6-oz.) glasses or ramekins. Sprinkle with crumbled cookies. Top with strawberries. Garnish, if desired. Serve immediately.

Note: We tested with Philadelphia Ready-To-Eat Cheesecake Filling and Biscoff cookies.

hip tip A **rubber stamp** with **mom's initials** is an inexpensive investment. Use it to personalize **cocktail napkins,** and send her home with a set of her own.

graduation party

menu

serves 12

Cilantro Guacamole

Fast Fajitas

Southwestern Salad

Ice Cream Bar

Whether it's a step up from high school, college, or even kindergarten, graduation day is a milestone worthy of a little hoopla. Throw a colorful get-together that shouts "fiesta!" to match the menu and the excitement of the day.

hostess
hit list:

The bulk of this menu relies upon prepared or pre-cooked packaged ingredients, leaving you plenty of time to set the stage.

The day before:

- Drain corn and chop tomato for salad; cover and chill
- Slice onions for fajitas; cover and chill

 ### 30 minutes before:

- Prepare guacamole; cover and chill
- Prepare fajitas

 ### 15 minutes before:

- Assemble salad
- Set up ice cream bar

Just before serving:

- Set out guacamole
- Remove ice cream from freezer

Cilantro Guacamole

makes 3¼ cups   hands-on time: 10 min.   total time: 10 min.

Cilantro spikes this beloved Mexican dip with fresh zest. Omit the herb if you're not a fan, and you'll still have great-tasting guacamole.

5   ripe avocados
⅓   cup chopped fresh cilantro
3   Tbsp. fresh lime juice
1   Tbsp. mayonnaise

1   tsp. salt
½   tsp. freshly ground pepper
1   garlic clove, pressed
Multigrain tortilla chips

1. Cut avocados in half. Scoop pulp into a bowl, and mash with a potato masher or fork until slightly chunky. Stir in cilantro and next 5 ingredients. Place plastic wrap directly on guacamole, and chill until ready to serve (up to 1 hour). Serve with tortilla chips.

"Roll and tie napkins like diplomas, insert accent flowers in clear vases, and use a paper tablecloth that guests can sign yearbook-style."

Fast Fajitas

makes 12 servings   hands-on time: 22 min.   total time: 30 min.

You'll have a little fajita seasoning mix leftover; stir it into ground beef for your next batch of burgers.

3   (17-oz.) packages fully cooked beef roast au jus
3   assorted bell peppers, cut into thin strips
2   Tbsp. vegetable oil
2   large sweet onions, sliced
1   lime, halved

1   (1.12-oz.) envelope fajita seasoning mix, divided
3   small tomatoes, cut into thin wedges
12   (6-inch) fajita-size flour tortillas, warmed
Garnish: lime wedges

1. Microwave roasts, one at a time, according to package directions.

2. Meanwhile, cook peppers in 1 Tbsp. hot vegetable oil in a large skillet over medium-high heat, stirring occasionally, 6 minutes or until tender and slightly charred. Cook onion in remaining 1 Tbsp. hot oil in another large skillet over medium-high heat, stirring occasionally, 10 minutes. Squeeze juice from half of lime over peppers and onions; sprinkle each with 1 tsp. seasoning mix, and toss to coat. Remove from heat; cover and keep warm.

2. Drain roasts, and place in a bowl, reserving 3 Tbsp. jus. Break meat into 1-inch chunks using a fork. Squeeze juice from remaining lime half over roast, and sprinkle with 1½ Tbsp. seasoning mix. Drizzle with reserved jus; toss gently. Place meat on a serving platter. Arrange peppers and onions around roast. Cover and keep warm.

3. Cook tomatoes in skillet over medium-high heat 2 to 3 minutes; sprinkle with ½ tsp. seasoning mix, and toss. Arrange tomatoes on serving platter. Serve with warm tortillas. Garnish, if desired.

Note: We tested with Hormel Fully Cooked Beef Roast Au Jus.

Southwestern Salad

makes 12 servings   hands-on time: 5 min.   total time: 5 min.

Blue corn tortilla chips give this crowd-pleasing salad some crunch.

3   (6.5-oz.) packages sweet butter lettuce
1½ cups (6 oz.) shredded Mexican four-cheese blend
1   (7- or 8-oz.) can Mexican-style corn, drained
1   large tomato, chopped

¾   cup Ranch dressing
¾   tsp. chili powder
¼   tsp. ground cumin
4   cups blue corn tortilla chips, coarsely crushed

1. Combine first 4 ingredients in a large salad bowl; toss. Combine dressing, chili powder, and cumin; drizzle over salad, and toss. Gently stir in crushed chips just before serving.

Note: We tested with Fresh Express Sweet Butter Lettuce.

Ice Cream Bar

makes 12 to 16 servings   hands-on time: 15 min.   total time: 15 min.

It goes without saying that you can tailor these ingredients, especially the ice cream, to suit your crowd. Gather a variety of mix-and-match serving bowls—borrow from a friend or relative if you need to.

½ dozen cinnamon rolls

½ (4-oz.) package ice cream cones

½ (14.7-oz.) package s'mores-flavored toaster pastries

6 (0.55-oz.) miniature peanut butter cup candies, chopped

4 (1.4-oz.) chocolate-covered toffee candy bars, coarsely crushed

3 (2.07-oz.) chocolate-covered caramel-peanut nougat bars, chopped

1 pt. fresh blueberries

1 pt. fresh strawberries, sliced

1 (7-oz.) container frozen strawberry cheesecake bites

1 (16-oz.) jar caramel topping, warmed

1 (16-oz.) jar hot fudge topping, warmed

1 (8.5-oz.) can refrigerated instant whipped cream

1 (10-oz.) jar whole maraschino cherries with stems, drained

2 (5-oz.) packages bear-shaped chewy candy

Rainbow candy sprinkles

1 gal. vanilla ice cream

1 gal. chocolate ice cream

1. Coarsely chop rolls; place in a serving bowl.

2. Coarsely crush 6 sugar cones to yield 1½ cups; place in a serving bowl. Chop 4 toaster pastries; place in a serving bowl. Place candy bars, fresh fruit, and cheesecake bites in serving bowls.

3. Arrange bowls of assorted toppings on serving table. Place warm toppings, whipped cream, cherries, bear-shaped chewy candy, and sprinkles on serving table.

4. Place ice cream containers in a large bowl of ice, if desired. Serve ice cream with assorted toppings.

Note: We tested with bakery cinnamon rolls, Keebler Sugar Cones, Kellogg's S'mores Pop Tarts, Reese's Peanut Butter Cup Candies, Heath Bars, Snickers Bars, Sara Lee Cheesecake Bites, Hershey's Caramel Topping, Hershey's Hot Fudge Topping, and Redi-Whip Instant Whipped Cream.

fast flourish Turn a roll of **wrapping paper** into a table runner. It makes for easy cleanup too.

father's day
breakfast

menu

serves 4 to 6

Honey-Ginger Fruit

Monterey Jack Omelets with Bacon, Avocado, and Salsa (double or triple recipe)

Lemon-Blueberry Muffins

cheese grits

orange juice/coffee

Stall him with a cup of coffee and the morning newspaper before he has a chance to get out of bed. Then you and the kids can take that extra time to get this bountiful breakfast on the table to show him just how much you care.

hostess
hit list:

Baskets, buckets, and bins keep the look casual for dad and hold everything from food to silverware to flowers. Gather them the night before the party.

The day before:

- Prep the fruit for the Honey-Ginger Fruit; cover and chill
- Bake muffins; store in an airtight container
- Set out napkins; line basket with napkin for muffins

30 minutes before:

- Pour juice into pitchers and place in refrigerator
- Set flowers on the table

15 minutes before:

- Prepare omelets
- Prepare cheese grits

Just before serving:

- Prepare Honey-Ginger Fruit
- Set out silverware

Honey-Ginger Fruit

makes 7 cups   hands-on time: 20 min.   total time: 20 min.

Grape juice, honey, and ginger add punch to whatever fruit you have on hand. Serve this fruit combo alone or over yogurt or warm biscuits.

1   cup white grape juice
3   Tbsp. honey
1½ tsp. grated fresh ginger
1   pt. fresh strawberries, halved

3   oranges, sectioned
½   honeydew melon, chopped
1   cup seedless green grapes

1. Combine grape juice, honey, and ginger in a large bowl. Add remaining ingredients, tossing to coat. Serve immediately.

Monterey Jack Omelets with Bacon, Avocado, and Salsa

makes 2 servings   hands-on time: 16 min.   total time: 16 min.

Pepper Jack cheese may be substituted for Monterey Jack if you prefer a spicier omelet.

6   fully-cooked bacon slices
1   cup (4 oz.) shredded Monterey Jack cheese
1   avocado, diced
¼   cup bottled salsa
¼   cup minced fresh cilantro

6   large eggs
½   tsp. salt
¼   tsp. freshly ground pepper
¼   cup butter

1. Reheat bacon according to package directions until crisp; coarsely crumble. Stir together bacon, ½ cup cheese, avocado, and salsa. Combine cilantro and remaining ½ cup cheese in a bowl.

2. Whisk together eggs, salt, pepper, and 2 Tbsp. water. Melt 2 Tbsp. butter in a 9-inch nonstick skillet over medium-high heat. Pour half of egg mixture into skillet, and sprinkle with half of cilantro-cheese mixture. As egg starts to cook, gently lift edges of omelet with a spatula, and tilt pan so uncooked portion flows underneath. Sprinkle 1 side of omelet with half of bacon mixture. Fold in half. Cook over medium-low heat 45 seconds. Remove from pan, and keep warm. Repeat procedure with remaining butter, egg mixture, cilantro-cheese mixture, and bacon mixture. Serve hot.

"Sprinkle Cheddar cheese over warm instant or quick-cooking grits just before serving.**"**

"Keep it casual by using an assortment of patterned and solid plates."

Lemon-Blueberry Muffins

makes 1 dozen   hands-on time: 10 min.   total time: 30 min.

Reheat muffins in the microwave 10 seconds or until warm.

1¾ cups all-purpose flour
2   tsp. baking powder
¼   tsp. salt
1   cup fresh or frozen blueberries, thawed and drained
¾   cup milk
½   cup sugar

¼   cup vegetable oil
2   tsp. lemon zest
1   tsp. vanilla extract
2   large eggs
Vegetable cooking spray

1. Preheat oven to 350°. Combine first 3 ingredients in a large bowl; add blueberries, and gently toss to coat. Make a well in center of mixture.

2. Stir together milk, sugar, and next 4 ingredients; add to dry ingredients, stirring just until moistened.

3. Spoon batter into 1 (12-cup) muffin pan coated with cooking spray, filling two-thirds full.

4. Bake at 350° for 20 to 25 minutes or until a wooden pick inserted in center comes out clean.

fourth of july

menu

serves 8

ribs from your favorite barbecue joint

Watermelon Barbecue Sauce

Tangy Blue Cheese Slaw

Blueberry Cobbler with Sugared Star Shortcakes

Independence Day is all about food, family, and fun spent outdoors.
A speedy cobbler and new twists on cookout favorites help make
pulling off a festive celebration a snap.

hostess
hit list:

This crowd-pleasing menu comes together quickly. Pick up slabs of ribs from a local barbecue restaurant to save time.

The day before:

- Prepare the barbecue sauce
- Bake the biscuit stars
- Set the table

30 minutes before:

- Pick up the ribs from the restaurant

15 minutes before:

- Prepare slaw
- Prepare cobbler mixture

Just before serving:

- Top cobbler with cream
- Place fruit in cups for table arrangements

Watermelon Barbecue Sauce

makes 3½ cups   hands-on time: 5 min.   total time: 5 min.

Pick up a slab or two of ribs from your favorite 'cue joint to serve with this sweet and zippy sauce.

3   cups chopped seedless watermelon
1   (18-oz.) bottle barbecue sauce

2   Tbsp. lemon juice

1. Process chopped watermelon in a food processor until blended. Stir together watermelon puree, barbecue sauce, and lemon juice.

Tangy Blue Cheese Slaw

makes 8 servings   hands-on time: 10 min.   total time: 10 min.

Don't be tempted to add more mayonnaise. Expect the dressing to lightly coat the slaw mix, and give it a toss just before serving.

½   cup white wine vinegar
¼   cup mayonnaise
¼   cup Dijon mustard
2   Tbsp. sugar
½   tsp. salt

½   tsp. pepper
2   (16-oz.) packages shredded coleslaw mix
4   green onions, sliced
1   (4-oz.) package crumbled blue cheese

1. Whisk together first 6 ingredients. Pour dressing over coleslaw mix and sliced green onions. Toss together, and top with crumbled blue cheese.

"You'll only need 3 cups of watermelon for the sauce, so plan to slice and serve the rest."

Blueberry Cobbler with Sugared Star Shortcakes

makes 10 servings   hands-on time: 10 min.   total time: 18 min.

Look for sparkling sugar at craft stores and supercenters. If you're in a pinch, granulated sugar is a good substitute. Reduce amount to 2 teaspoons.

2   pt. fresh blueberries
½   cup granulated sugar
1   Tbsp. lemon juice
⅛   tsp. almond extract

2   (12-oz.) cans refrigerated buttermilk biscuits
1   Tbsp. coarse sparkling sugar
Sweetened whipped cream

1. Preheat oven to 400°. Combine first 4 ingredients in a medium saucepan. Cook over medium-high heat 5 minutes or until bubbly and sugar dissolves. Remove from heat.

2. Separate biscuits, and flatten each into a 3½-inch circle. Cut with a 3-inch star-shaped cutter, and place on a lightly greased baking sheet; sprinkle with sparkling sugar, pressing to adhere. Bake at 400° for 8 minutes or until lightly browned.

3. Spoon blueberry mixture into 10 bowls; top with biscuits. Serve with whipped cream.

Note: We tested with Pillsbury Grands! Jr. Golden Layers Buttermilk Biscuits.

birthday party

menu

serves 6

Instant Gazpacho

Couscous with Peas and Feta

Grilled Grouper with Orange-Almond Sauce

Limoncello Trifle

Turn the spotlight on a dear friend or family member on their birthday by hosting a colorful fête fit for a king or queen. Make it personal with old photos, a station for guests to create their own gift for the honoree, and a supply of fun factoids about the other events that happened on this day in history.

hostess
hit list:

This menu is all about the big chill. The flavors of make-ahead dishes, such as the gazpacho and couscous salad, really come together in the refrigerator, giving you more time for the decorating fun.

The day before:

- Prepare gazpacho; cover and chill
- Prepare couscous; cover and chill
- Make trifle; cover and chill

30 minutes before:

- Prepare grouper and sauce

Just before serving:

- Stir pine nuts into couscous to serve
- Pour drinks

Instant Gazpacho

makes 5½ cups   hands-on time: 15 min.   total time: 15 min.

5   green onions, sliced
1   small red bell pepper, diced
1   small cucumber, diced
2   plum tomatoes, diced

3   cups Bloody Mary mix
¼   tsp. salt
¼   tsp. pepper

1. Stir together all ingredients. Cover and chill until ready to serve. Ladle soup into bowls.

Couscous with Peas and Feta

makes 6 servings   hands-on time: 10 min.   total time: 25 min.

Toasted pine nuts and tangy feta give this cool side dish plenty of personality.

1   cup uncooked plain couscous
2   Tbsp. pine nuts
¼   cup olive oil
1   tsp. lemon zest
1   Tbsp. fresh lemon juice
¾   tsp. kosher salt

⅛   tsp. ground red pepper
¾   cup frozen sweet green peas, thawed
½   cup finely chopped red onion
½   cup crumbled feta cheese
¼   cup chopped fresh mint

1. Bring 1½ cups water to a boil in a saucepan over high heat. Remove from heat, and stir in couscous; let stand 10 minutes.
2. Meanwhile, heat pine nuts in a small skillet over medium-low heat, stirring often, 5 minutes or until toasted and fragrant.
3. Stir together olive oil, lemon zest, and next 3 ingredients. Transfer couscous to a large bowl. Add olive oil mixture to couscous, stirring with a fork. Add peas, chopped onion, crumbled feta, and chopped mint, and toss gently; cover and chill until ready to serve. Stir in pine nuts just before serving.

"Mix it up. For an eclectic feel, use mismatched china and linens in an array of colors."

Grilled Grouper with Orange-Almond Sauce

makes 6 servings   hands-on time: 20 min.   total time: 20 min.

6   (8-oz.) grouper fillets
2   Tbsp. olive oil
1   tsp. coarse-grain sea salt
1   tsp. freshly ground pepper
Vegetable cooking spray

½   cup butter
½   cup sliced almonds
1   Tbsp. orange zest
Garnish: fresh thyme sprigs*

1. Rub fish fillets with oil. Sprinkle with salt and pepper.

2. Coat cold cooking grate of grill with cooking spray, and place on grill. Preheat grill to 400° to 500° (high) heat. Place fish on cooking grate, and grill, covered with grill lid, 5 to 6 minutes on each side or until fish flakes with a fork.

3. Melt butter in a saucepan over medium-high heat; add almonds, and sauté 5 minutes or until butter is brown. Remove from heat. Stir in orange zest. Pour sauce over fish. Garnish, if desired.

*Orange thyme sprigs may be substituted.

hip tip The guest of honor will appreciate personal touches such as **old photos** and one-of-a-kind **gifts** created by friends.

Limoncello Trifle

makes 10 to 12 servings   hands-on time: 10 min.   total time: 30 min.

1   (40-oz.) store-bought vanilla pound cake
1   (8-oz.) package mascarpone cheese
1   (10-oz.) jar lemon curd
2   (4-oz.) vanilla instant pudding cups

⅔   cup limoncello, well chilled
2½ cups thawed, frozen whipped topping
Garnish: lemon zest

1. Cut pound cake into bite-size pieces to yield 6 cups. Reserve remaining cake for another use. Place half of cake cubes in a 2½-qt. trifle bowl.

2. Combine cheese, lemon curd, and vanilla pudding, stirring well.

3. Drizzle ⅓ cup limoncello over cake in bowl. Spoon 1¼ cups lemon curd mixture over cake. Top with 1 cup whipped topping. Repeat layers once, ending with remaining 1½ cups whipped topping. Chill 20 minutes to 24 hours. Garnish, if desired.

tree-trimming party

menu

serves 8

Super Quick Chili

Cornmeal Scones with Sage and Cheddar

Cookie S'mores

Hot Mocha

The most memorable gift of all is a great time, so gather friends in your home to decorate the tree. Serve up a soul-satisfying meal of comfort foods that will keep guests toasty as everyone adds a bit of sparkle and cheer to your freshly-cut evergreen.

hostess
hit list:

Planning a holiday party couldn't be any easier. While the chili simmers, prepare the scones. Set a festive mood by playing some cool Christmas tunes.

The day before:

- Make cookies; cover
- Prepare chili toppings and chill

30 minutes before:

- Prepare chili
- Prepare scones

15 minutes before:

- Prepare Hot Mochas

Just before serving:

- Assemble cookies, and broil marshmallows
- Top mochas with cream and chocolate syrup

Super Quick Chili

makes 8 servings   hands-on time: 27 min.   total time: 27 min.

2   lb. lean ground beef
2   Tbsp. chili powder
1   Tbsp. Creole seasoning
1   tsp. ground cumin
2   (16-oz.) cans diced tomatoes with green peppers
     and onion

2   (16-oz.) cans small red beans
2   (8-oz.) cans tomato sauce
Toppings: shredded Cheddar cheese, sliced green
     onions, diced tomatoes

1. Brown beef in a Dutch oven over medium-high heat, stirring often, 6 to 8 minutes or until beef crumbles and is no longer pink; drain well. Return beef to Dutch oven; sprinkle with chili powder, Creole seasoning, and cumin, and sauté 1 minute.

2. Stir in diced tomatoes and next 2 ingredients, and bring to a boil over medium-high heat, stirring occasionally. Cover, reduce heat to low, and simmer, stirring occasionally, 15 minutes. Serve with toppings.

Cornmeal Scones with Sage and Cheddar

makes 10 servings   hands-on time: 13 min.   total time: 30 min.

1⅔ cups all-purpose flour
⅓   cup plain yellow cornmeal
2½ tsp. baking powder
1   tsp. rubbed sage
½   tsp. salt

⅛   tsp. ground red pepper
½   cup cold butter, cut into small pieces
1   cup (4 oz.) shredded Cheddar cheese
½   cup milk
1   large egg, lightly beaten

1. Preheat oven to 400°. Combine flour and next 5 ingredients in a large bowl. Cut in butter with a pastry blender or 2 knives until mixture resembles coarse meal. Stir in cheese. Add milk and egg, stirring just until dry ingredients are moistened.

2. Turn dough out onto a lightly floured surface, and knead 3 or 4 times. Transfer dough to a lightly greased baking sheet; pat into a 7-inch circle. Cut into 10 wedges, cutting to but not through bottom of dough. (Do not separate wedges.)

3. Bake at 400° for 17 minutes or until golden. Transfer scones to a wire rack. Serve warm.

Cookie S'mores

makes 8 servings   hands-on time: 10 min.
total time: 13 min.

16 bakery cookies
1   (4-oz.) bittersweet chocolate baking bar
8   large marshmallows

1. Preheat broiler with oven rack 6 inches from heat.
Separate chocolate bar into 8 squares. Place 1
chocolate square on flat side of each of 8 cookies.
2. Place marshmallows on a baking sheet. Broil 3
minutes or until puffed and toasted. Immediately
transfer marshmallows to tops of chocolate squares,
using a small spatula. Top marshmallows with
remaining cookies, flat sides down; press down gently.
Note: We tested with Ghiradelli Chocolate Baking Bar.

hostess helper Strapped for time?
You can also top the flat side of **the cookies**
with a piece of chocolate and the marshmallow. "Roast" the marshmallow with a
match-stick lighter, and sandwich with the
other cookie.

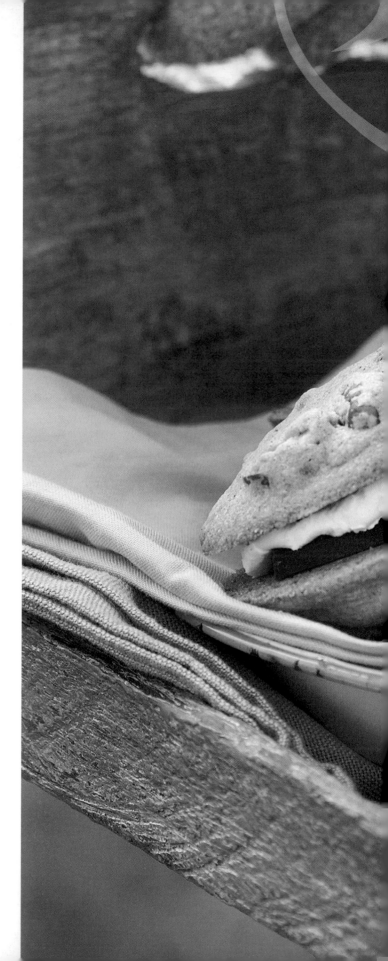

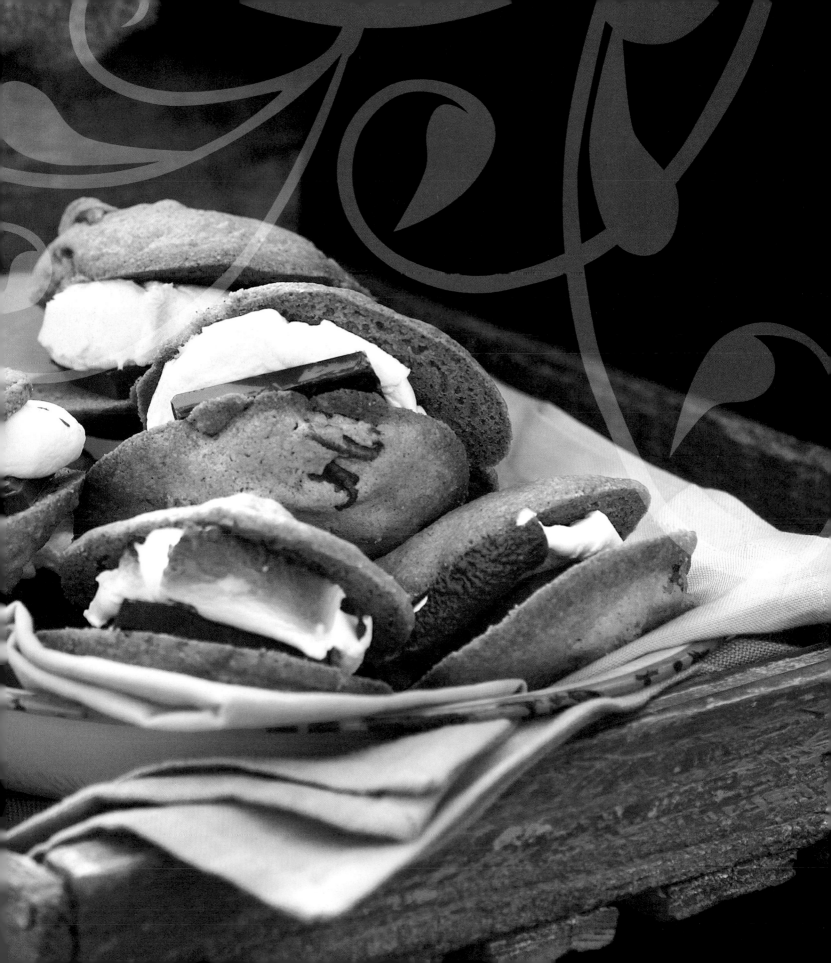

hip tip Ornaments are tucked into these perfectly rustic takeaways that have been personalized for guests with stick-on initials and sealed with a clothespin and twine.

Hot Mocha

makes about 10 cups   hands-on time: 15 min.   total time: 15 min.

Whether you mix the Hot Mudslide version (see variation) or the nonalcoholic one, this comforting drink will warm you down to your toes. Omit espresso or substitute decaffeinated espresso for the youngsters.

2   cups half-and-half

1   cup unsweetened cocoa

1   cup sugar

¼   cup instant espresso

6   cups milk

4   tsp. vanilla extract

Sweetened whipped cream

Chocolate syrup

1. Whisk together first 4 ingredients in a large saucepan. Cook, whisking constantly, over medium heat 2 to 3 minutes or until sugar dissolves. Whisk in milk; cook over medium-high heat, whisking constantly, 5 minutes or until very hot. (Do not boil.) Whisk in vanilla.

2. Pour chocolate mixture into mugs; top with whipped cream, and drizzle with chocolate syrup.

Hot Mudslide: Omit espresso. Stir ½ cup coffee liqueur, ½ cup Irish cream liqueur, and, if desired, ¼ cup vodka into hot milk mixture with vanilla. Proceed as directed.

Note: We tested with Kahlúa and Bailey's Irish Crème.

"Thick-walled mugs keep drinks warm longer. A drizzle of chocolate syrup on top is both tasty and pretty.**"**

christmas eve
supper

menu

serves 6

Quick Cheese Tray

Skillet Lasagna

Caesar-Style Salad

Parmesan Breadsticks

bakery bûche de noël

For many families the night-before-Christmas meal is the special one that is shared with extended family and friends, but that doesn't have to mean more pressure for the hostess. This menu impresses with easy Italian favorites, so you can focus on your loved ones.

hostess
hit list:

Raid your grocery store for Italian delicacies for the cheese tray, breadstick dough for the Parmesan Sticks, and a special holiday pastry from the bakery. Buon appetito!

The day before:

- Combine first 3 ingredients for breadsticks; cover and chill
- Make salad dressing; cover and chill

 ### 30 minutes before:

- Prepare and bake breadsticks
- Prepare Skillet Lasagna

15 minutes before:

- Prepare cheese tray
- Prepare salad

Just before serving:

- Let lasagna stand, and garnish with basil
- Toss salad with dressing to serve
- Place dessert on serving dish

Quick Cheese Tray

makes 8 servings   hands-on time: 10 min.   total time: 10 min.

Many times the grocery store will let you taste different cheeses or offer suggestions. Look to the salad bar for a variety of olives.

Niçoise, kalamata, cerignola, or picholine olives
1   (8-oz.) wedge fontina cheese
2   Fuyu persimmons, sliced

2   pears, thinly sliced
¼   lb. thinly sliced prosciutto
    Ciabatta bread, sliced

1. Arrange all ingredients on a large serving platter or cutting board.

Party Tip: Fuyu persimmons, which are a beautiful red-orange fruit, are available October through February. Shaped like a tomato, they have a super-sweet melon-like flavor. Fuyus should be eaten while still firm and crisp versus the Hachiya, another type that should be enjoyed when the fruit is very soft.

"Make it memorable. Flickering candles and votives displayed in a variety of ways are bound to scream 'merry and bright.' Be creative!"

Skillet Lasagna

makes 6 servings   hands-on time: 18 min.   total time: 28 min.

1   cup chopped onion
1   tsp. minced garlic
1   Tbsp. olive oil
1   (24-oz.) jar tomato-and-basil pasta sauce
½   (12-oz.) package extra-wide egg noodles

¼   tsp. salt
¼   tsp. dried crushed red pepper
½   cup low-fat ricotta cheese
1   cup (4 oz.) shredded Italian six-cheese blend
2   Tbsp. chopped fresh basil (optional)

1. Sauté onion and garlic in hot oil in a 10-inch skillet over medium heat 5 minutes or until vegetables are tender. Stir in pasta sauce, egg noodles, and 1 cup water. Bring to a boil; reduce heat to medium to medium-low, and simmer, stirring occasionally, 8 to 10 minutes or until pasta is just tender and liquid is almost absorbed. Stir in salt and crushed red pepper.

2. Stir together ricotta and ½ cup shredded cheese. Drop by heaping tablespoonfuls over pasta. Sprinkle with remaining ½ cup cheese.

3. Cook, covered, over low heat 5 minutes or until thoroughly heated and cheese is melted. Remove from heat, and let stand 5 minutes. Sprinkle with basil, if desired.

Note: We tested with Classico Tomato & Basil Pasta Sauce.

> "Serve food family-style...the traditional Italian way. Keeping it casual makes the hostess's job easier too!"

Caesar-Style Salad

makes 6 servings   hands-on time: 10 min.   total time: 10 min.

Try with cooked cheese tortellini, or top with grilled chicken or shrimp.

½ cup olive oil

⅓ cup fresh lemon juice

2 garlic cloves, pressed

1 tsp. Worcestershire sauce

¾ tsp. kosher salt

½ tsp. freshly ground pepper

1 (2-lb.) package torn romaine lettuce

½ cup freshly shaved or shredded Parmesan cheese

1 cup large plain croutons

1. Whisk together first 6 ingredients.

2. Place lettuce in a large bowl. Pour olive oil mixture over lettuce, and toss. Sprinkle with cheese, tossing to combine. Top with croutons, and serve immediately.

Make Ahead Note: Olive oil mixture may be prepared up to 24 hours ahead. Cover and chill until ready to serve. Whisk before serving.

Time Shaver: Substitute a bottled Caesar dressing for the first 6 ingredients, if you'd like.

Parmesan Breadsticks

makes 1 dozen   hands-on time: 10 min.   total time: 21 min.

¼ cup freshly grated Parmesan cheese

½ tsp. dried parsley flakes

¼ tsp. garlic powder

1 (11-oz.) can refrigerated breadsticks

3 Tbsp. butter, melted

Salt to taste

1. Preheat oven to 375°. Combine first 3 ingredients.

2. Separate dough, and twist each piece into a 10-inch rope. Brush with melted butter, and sprinkle with cheese mixture. Place on a lightly greased baking sheet.

3. Bake at 375° for 11 to 13 minutes or until golden. Sprinkle with salt to taste.

new year's eve

menu

serves 8

Champagne and cranberries

Shrimp Shooters

Red Pepper Jelly-Brie Bites

Country Ham Mini Biscuits

Welcome the New Year in high style. Pull out all the stops with confetti, tantalizing finger foods, sparkling Champagne cocktails, and glittering silver accents. The food might be quick and easy, but this affair is nothing but elegant.

hostess
hit list:

A palette of shimmering silver and white provides the perfect backdrop for fancy foods downsized to pick-up proportions. A combo of make-ahead and bake-to-serve offerings makes this soirée simple to execute.

The day before:

- Prepare shrimp; cover and chill
- Prepare Black Pepper Honey

30 minutes before:

- Bake biscuits

15 minutes before:

- Prepare brie bites

Just before serving:

- Assemble shooters
- Assemble mini biscuits
- Pour cocktails (drop a few dried cranberries in each glass before pouring Champagne)

Shrimp Shooters

makes 8 servings   hands-on time: 15 min.   **total time: 15 min.**, plus 1 day for chilling

You can chill the shrimp for 8 hours, if desired.

⅔ cup olive oil

½ cup white balsamic vinegar

1 Tbsp. chopped fresh cilantro

2 Tbsp. lemon zest

1 tsp. salt

1 tsp. freshly ground pepper

1 tsp. hot sauce

1½ lb. peeled, large cooked shrimp

Romaine lettuce heart leaves, separated into leaves

1. Whisk together olive oil and next 6 ingredients in a large bowl.

2. Place cooked shrimp and vinaigrette mixture in a large zip-top plastic freezer bag. Seal and chill 24 hours, turning bag occasionally.

3. Arrange lettuce leaves in 8 (6- to 8-oz.) glasses. Spoon shrimp mixture into glasses.

Make Ahead Note: Vinaigrette may be prepared ahead and stored in an airtight container in the refrigerator up to 1 week. Let vinaigrette come to room temperature, and whisk before adding cooked shrimp.

fast flourish Let **small-scale cups** and **glasses** work double duty. Wrap with ribbon, fill with confetti and candles, or pack with pickled shrimp for a modern touch.

Red Pepper Jelly-Brie Bites

makes 30 tartlets   hands-on time: 10 min.   total time: 15 min.

2   (1.9-oz.) packages frozen mini-phyllo pastry shells, thawed

3   oz. Brie cheese, rind removed

8   tsp. red pepper jelly

3   Tbsp. chopped roasted salted almonds

1. Preheat oven to 350°. Place mini-phyllo pastry shells on a baking sheet. Cut Brie cheese into 30 very small pieces. Spoon ¼ rounded teaspoonful red pepper jelly into each shell; top with cheese. Sprinkle with almonds. Bake tartlets 5 to 6 minutes or until cheese is melted.

Country Ham Mini Biscuits

makes 24 appetizers   hands-on time: 5 min.   total time: 20 min., including honey

1   (24-oz.) package frozen mini biscuits (24 biscuits)

1   (8-oz.) package thinly sliced country ham

Black Pepper Honey

1. Bake biscuits according to package directions.

2. Fill biscuits with ham. Serve with Black Pepper Honey.

Note: We tested with Mary B's Bite-Sized Buttermilk Tea Biscuits.

black pepper honey

makes ½ cup   hands-on time: 5 min.   total time: 5 min.

½   cup honey

2   tsp. coarsely ground pepper

2   dashes of hot sauce

1. Stir together all ingredients in a small bowl until blended.

> **"**I love serving bite-size foods. It allows guests to nibble while they mingle.**"**

chic
soirées

Whether you're a little bit country or a little bit rock and roll, sometimes you want to party in high style. So break out the china and pop the Champagne— the parties on the following pages give you lots of ways to celebrate.

rush hour shower

menu

serves 6

Raspberry Beer Cocktail

Simple Antipasto Platter

Greek Caesar Salad

Shrimp-Pesto Pizza or Chicken Alfredo Pizza

Brandy-Vanilla Cheesecake Dip

Throwing a party after work is easy when it's tackled the Half-Hour Hostess way. Your choice of one or two gourmet-style pizzas and a few quick-to-come-together appetizers make it look like you've been in the kitchen all day. Instead, you can let the stress of the workday roll away while you and your friends have fun.

hostess
hit list:

Liven up a palette of dusty pastels with punches of tangerine for a fresh, modern look that's repeated in the food, flowers, and decor.

The day before:

- Roll goat cheese in parsley for antipasto platter; cover and chill
- Prepare Caesar dressing for salad; cover and chill
- Prepare pizza dough for one or both pizzas according to note on either pizza recipe
- Peel and devein shrimp if making Shrimp-Pesto Pizza
- Prepare cheesecake dip; cover and chill

30 minutes before:

- Assemble antipasto platter
- Prepare pizzas

15 minutes before:

- Assemble and dress salad
- Arrange dip on serving platter with fruit and cookies

 ### Just before serving:

- Stir together cocktail, and pour over ice
- Give a toast, and clink glasses

Raspberry Beer Cocktail

makes 6 servings   hands-on time: 5 min.   **total time: 5 min.**

You can use fresh raspberries, but frozen taste just as good. Make a big batch for a larger crowd.

¾ cup frozen raspberries*
3½ (12-oz.) bottles beer, chilled
1 (12-oz.) container frozen raspberry lemonade
   concentrate, thawed

½ cup vodka
Garnish: lemon and lime slices

1. Stir together first 4 ingredients. Serve over ice. Garnish, if desired.
*Fresh raspberries may be substituted.
Make Ahead Note: Stir together lemonade concentrate and vodka in a large container. Chill up to 3 days.
Stir in raspberries and beer just before serving. Garnish, if desired.

Simple Antipasto Platter

makes 8 servings   hands-on time: 10 min.   **total time: 10 min.**

Antipasto platters are crowd-pleasers and can be as minimal or grand as you care to make them. Other
worthy additions: Spanish olives, marinated artichoke hearts, and fresh mozzarella.

1 (5-oz.) goat cheese log
2 Tbsp. chopped fresh parsley
1 (16-oz.) jar pickled okra, drained
1 (8-oz.) jar kalamata olives, drained and rinsed

1 (7-oz.) jar roasted red bell peppers, drained and
   cut into pieces
4 oz. sliced salami
Assorted crackers and breadsticks

1. Roll goat cheese log in parsley; place on a serving platter. Arrange okra and next 3 ingredients on platter
around goat cheese. Serve with assorted crackers and breadsticks.

> **"**Don't be afraid to use what you already
> have on hand in new ways. An old flour crock
> instantly becomes a punch bowl when paired
> with a soup ladle for serving.**"**

"Set up a 'wish' jar for the bride-to-be so that she can leave with good tidings from her closest pals to read later.**"**

Greek Caesar Salad

makes 6 servings   hands-on time: 10 min.   **total time: 10 min.**

¾ cup olive oil
¼ cup lemon juice
¼ cup egg substitute
2   garlic cloves, pressed
1   tsp. dried oregano
¼ tsp. salt

⅛ tsp. pepper
1   head romaine lettuce, torn
¾ cup kalamata olives
1   small red onion, thinly sliced
½ cup crumbled feta cheese
Croutons

1. Whisk together olive oil and next 6 ingredients in a small bowl. Cover and chill up to 2 days.
2. Combine lettuce and next 3 ingredients in a large bowl; gradually add enough olive oil mixture to coat leaves, tossing gently. Sprinkle with croutons, and serve with remaining olive oil mixture.

Shrimp-Pesto Pizza

makes 6 servings   hands-on time: 30 min.   **total time: 30 min.**

We found fresh pizza dough available behind the bakery counter at the grocery store. If you're expecting a larger crowd, you can buy pizza dough in bulk from your local wholesale club or even a favorite pizza restaurant.

Vegetable cooking spray
1   lb. peeled and deveined, large raw shrimp
    (31/35 count)
1   cup refrigerated prechopped yellow onion
1   red bell pepper, chopped
¼   tsp. salt
¼   tsp. pepper

2   Tbsp. olive oil
1½ lb. bakery pizza dough
All-purpose flour
Plain yellow cornmeal
½   cup jarred refrigerated pesto
¾   cup freshly grated Parmesan cheese

1. Coat cold cooking grate of grill with cooking spray, and place on grill. Preheat grill to 350° (medium) heat.

2. Peel shrimp, and slice in half lengthwise; devein, if desired.

3. Sauté onion, bell pepper, salt, and pepper in 1 Tbsp. hot oil in a large skillet over medium heat 5 minutes or until tender. Transfer onion mixture to a large bowl. Sauté shrimp in remaining 1 Tbsp. hot oil 3 minutes or just until shrimp turn pink. Add shrimp to onion mixture, and toss.

4. Divide dough into 6 equal portions. Lightly sprinkle flour on a large surface. Roll each portion into a 6-inch round (about ¼-inch thick). Carefully transfer pizza dough rounds to a cutting board or baking sheet sprinkled with cornmeal.

5. Slide pizza dough rounds onto cooking grate of grill; spread pesto over rounds, and top with shrimp mixture. Sprinkle each with 2 Tbsp. Parmesan cheese.

6. Grill, covered with grill lid, 4 minutes. Rotate pizzas one-quarter turn, and grill, covered with grill lid, 5 to 6 more minutes or until pizza crusts are cooked. Serve immediately.

Make Ahead Note: Individual pizza dough rounds may be made ahead. Roll out as directed, and place between pieces of wax paper sprinkled with flour and cornmeal; place in a gallon-size zip-top plastic bag. Seal bag, and chill up to 8 hours.

Chicken Alfredo Pizza

makes 6 servings   hands-on time: 29 min.   **total time: 29 min.**

A deli-roasted garlic- and herb-flavored rotisserie chicken is an easy shortcut for chopped cooked chicken.

Vegetable cooking spray

¾ cup refrigerated Alfredo sauce

1½ lb. bakery pizza dough

All-purpose flour

Plain yellow cornmeal

1 (6-oz.) package fresh baby spinach

2 cups chopped cooked chicken

1½ cups (6 oz.) shredded fontina cheese

2 tsp. lemon juice

¼ tsp. salt

¼ tsp. pepper

1. Coat cold cooking grate of grill with cooking spray, and place on grill. Preheat grill to 350° (medium) heat.

2. Heat Alfredo sauce in a saucepan over medium-low heat; keep warm.

3. Divide dough into 6 equal portions. Lightly sprinkle flour on a large surface. Roll each portion into a 6-inch round (about ¼-inch thick). Carefully transfer pizza dough rounds to a cutting board or baking sheet sprinkled with cornmeal.

4. Slide pizza dough rounds onto cooking grate of grill; spread Alfredo sauce over rounds, and top with spinach, chicken, and cheese. Sprinkle with lemon juice, salt, and pepper.

5. Grill, covered with grill lid, 4 minutes. Rotate pizzas one-quarter turn, and grill, covered with grill lid, 5 to 6 more minutes or until pizza crusts are cooked. Serve immediately.

Make Ahead Note: Individual pizza dough rounds may be made ahead. Roll out as directed, and place between pieces of wax paper sprinkled with flour and cornmeal; place in a gallon-size zip-top plastic bag. Seal bag, and chill up to 8 hours.

Note: We tested with Buitoni Alfredo Sauce.

"In a pinch, I have substituted self-rising cornmeal mix—you know, the kind you use to make cornbread—for plain yellow cornmeal. But shhh…don't tell anyone."

Brandy-Vanilla Cheesecake Dip

makes 3 cups   hands-on time: 5 min.   **total time: 5 min.**

Refrigerated cheesecake filling is sold in a tub near the cream cheese. It is fully cooked and ready to use.

1   (24.2-oz.) container ready-to-eat cheesecake filling
5   Tbsp. brandy

1   tsp. vanilla extract
Assorted fruit and cookies

1. Stir together first 3 ingredients. Cover and chill until ready to serve. Serve with assorted fruit and cookies.
Note: We tested with Philadelphia Ready-To-Eat Cheesecake Filling.

celebrate spring
brunch

menu

serves 8 to 10

Champagne mimosas

Quick Strata

Minted Melon Salad with Pancetta

Cinnamon-Sugar Pecan Scones

Grilled Doughnuts

Spring is the perfect time to open your doors and reconnect with friends over a weekend brunch. Keeping the menu simple is key. Once you see how easy it is with a few shortcuts, it's sure to become an annual affair.

hostess
hit list:

Layer pastel linens for a pretty spring table, and toast friendship over girlie mimosas— glasses of Champagne with a splash of orange juice.

The day before:

- Make melon salad, reserving pancetta; chill
- Prepare scones; let cool. Store in airtight container
- Cut strawberries for Grilled Doughnuts

30 minutes before:

- Prepare strata

15 minutes before:

- Grill doughnuts

Just before serving:

- Sprinkle salad with pancetta, and garnish
- Reheat scones in microwave oven
- Pour mimosas as guests arrive

Quick Strata

makes 8 servings   hands-on time: 10 min.   **total time: 30 min.**

Bake this brunch egg dish in two pie plates to get it to the table even faster.

7   (¾-inch-thick) ciabatta bread slices
5   large eggs
½   cup whipping cream
½   cup half-and-half
½   cup refrigerated prechopped onion

1   (8-oz.) package shredded Mexican four-cheese blend
½   (8-oz.) package shredded Monterey Jack cheese
1   (4.5-oz.) can chopped green chiles, drained
1   (2-oz.) jar diced pimiento, drained

1. Preheat oven to 425°. Tear bread into bite-size pieces to equal 6 cups, firmly packed.

2. Combine eggs and remaining ingredients in a large bowl; gently stir in bread. Pour bread mixture into lightly greased 9-inch deep dish pie plates.

3. Bake at 425° for 20 to 22 minutes or until browned and set. Serve immediately.

Shopping Tip: Look for prechopped onion in the refrigerated produce section.

Minted Melon Salad with Pancetta

makes 8 to 10 servings   hands-on time: 14 min.   **total time: 30 min.**

Making and chilling this salad in advance allows for a more pronounced flavor.

3   oz. thinly sliced pancetta or prosciutto
3   Tbsp. sugar
1   Tbsp. finely chopped crystallized ginger
⅛   tsp. ground red pepper

2   fresh mint sprigs
8   cups cubed cantaloupe
1   cup fresh blueberries
2   Tbsp. chopped fresh mint

1. Cook pancetta in a nonstick skillet over medium-high heat 4 to 6 minutes or until crisp. Remove from heat; coarsely crumble.

2. Combine sugar, next 3 ingredients, and ⅓ cup water in a small saucepan. Bring to a boil over medium-high heat; boil 3 minutes or until slightly syrupy. Remove from heat; cool to room temperature (about 5 minutes), and pour through a strainer into a bowl; discard solids. Cover and chill 5 minutes.

3. Combine cantaloupe and blueberries in a serving bowl. Drizzle with chilled syrup mixture; toss gently. Add 2 Tbsp. mint. Serve immediately, or cover and chill until ready to serve (up to 24 hours). Sprinkle with pancetta just before serving.

Cinnamon-Sugar Pecan Scones

makes 14 servings   hands-on time: 12 min.   **total time: 30 min.**

Mounding scoops of dough on baking sheets takes the fussiness out of this traditionally upscale dough.

3 cups all-purpose flour

⅔ cup granulated sugar

1 Tbsp. baking powder

2 tsp. ground cinnamon

½ tsp. salt

¾ cup cold unsalted butter, cut into pieces

1½ cups chopped pecans, toasted

1 large egg

1 cup whipping cream

1 tsp. vanilla extract

Parchment paper

2 Tbsp. whipping cream or half-and-half

2 Tbsp. granulated sugar or cinnamon sugar

1. Preheat oven to 425°. Stir together first 5 ingredients in a large bowl; cut in butter with a pastry blender until crumbly. Stir in pecans.

2. Whisk together egg, 1 cup cream, and vanilla; add to dry ingredients, stirring with a fork just until mixture forms a shaggy dough. Scoop dough onto parchment paper-lined baking sheets using a ⅓-cup measuring cup. Brush tops with 2 Tbsp. cream; sprinkle with 2 Tbsp. sugar.

3. Bake at 425° for 18 minutes or until browned. Serve warm.

fast flourish Vintage-looking **glasses** can double as beautiful vases for small centerpieces.

Grilled Doughnuts

makes 8 to 10 servings   hands-on time: 14 min.
total time: 14 min.

A large skillet works pan-grilled magic on simple store-bought doughnuts. These lightly crisped, caramelized doughnuts are crazy good—and fun at any age for breakfast, brunch, or dessert.

6   glazed doughnuts
Vegetable cooking spray
1½ cups fresh strawberries, halved
Powdered sugar

1. Cut each doughnut in half lengthwise.
2. Heat a large nonstick skillet over medium heat; coat lightly with cooking spray. Place doughnut halves, 4 at a time, cut sides down, in skillet. Cook 2 to 4 minutes or until toasted. Cool slightly; cut each grilled doughnut half into 2 pieces. Repeat with remaining doughnuts. Serve with strawberries sprinkled with sugar.
Note: We tested with Krispy Kreme doughnuts.

quick finds Consignment shops, flea markets, and yes, even grandma's closet, are great places to look for dainty **antique platters** and **bowls**.

southwest supper

menu

serves 8

Pomegranate Margaritas

your favorite salsa, tortilla chips, and queso fresco

Mixed Grill with Cilantro Pesto

Creamy Black Bean-and-Rice Bake

Southwestern Salad with Candied Pumpkin Seeds

Trés Leches Trifles with Summer Berries

You're bound to receive rave reviews when guests try this ruby spin on everyone's favorite cocktail, the margarita. Rub glass rims with a lime wedge, and invert; then dip and twist each in a container of margarita salt to serve classically. Complete the festive tone by marching votive and pillar candles down the center of the table between an unexpected "runner" of rocks and stones.

hostess
hit list:

Traditionally served over refried beans, tacos, and enchiladas, a sprinkle of salty-delicious queso fresco is a nice addition to the usual chips and salsa. Let guests nibble and sip while you get the main event ready.

The day before:

- Toast pumpkin seeds for salad and pesto
- Prepare cilantro pesto; cover and chill
- Prepare candied pumpkin seeds; store in airtight container
- Prepare trifles; cover and chill
- Prepare step 1 of Pomegranate Margaritas; cover and chill

🕐 30 minutes before:

- Prepare Mixed Grill
- Prepare bean and rice bake

🕐 15 minutes before:

- Dip rims of cocktail glasses in margarita salt, if desired
- Set out salsa, chips, and cheese

🕐 Just before serving:

- Shake and pour cocktails
- Assemble salad to serve

Pomegranate Margaritas

makes 8 servings   hands-on time: 20 min.   **total time: 20 min.**

Using tequila labeled *plata*, or silver, balances the tart flavors of pomegranate and lime juices.

½ cup sugar

½ cup hot water

3 cups pomegranate juice

1½ cups tequila

1 cup fresh lime juice (about 12 limes)

½ cup orange liqueur

Garnish: orange and lime slices

1. Stir together sugar and hot water until sugar is dissolved. Stir in pomegranate juice and next 3 ingredients.

2. Pour desired amount of pomegranate juice mixture into a cocktail shaker filled with ice cubes. Cover with lid, and shake 30 seconds or until thoroughly chilled. Remove lid, and strain into chilled cocktail glasses. Repeat procedure with remaining pomegranate mixture. Garnish, if desired. Serve immediately.

Note: We tested with Triple Sec orange liqueur.

fast flourish **Banana leaves** add depth and interest to platters, and are fun to use for any occasion. They are available fresh or frozen at Asian markets.

Mixed Grill with Cilantro Pesto

makes 8 servings   hands-on time: 21 min.   **total time: 26 min.,** not including pesto

When offering a mixed grill, cut each chop and steak in half so that guests can try both. Feel free to offer only pork or beef, just buy eight pieces of meat—one for each guest. For great grill marks, don't try to move the meat (even a little!) until the end of the cooking time.

4   (1½-inch-thick) center-cut bone-in pork chops
4   (6-oz.) beef tenderloin fillets (about 2 inches thick)
Kosher salt

Pepper
Cilantro Pesto

1. Preheat grill to 350° to 400° (medium-high) heat. Sprinkle pork chops and beef fillets with desired amount of salt and pepper.
2. Grill chops and fillets, covered with grill lid. Grill chops for 8 to 10 minutes on each side or until done. Grill fillets 8 to 10 minutes. Turn fillets over, and cook 5 more minutes or to desired degree of doneness. Remove chops and fillets from grill, and let stand 5 minutes. Serve with Cilantro Pesto.

cilantro pesto

makes about ¾ cup   hands-on time: 10 min.   **total time: 10 min.**

This pesto has a rougher, drier consistency than traditional ones. For a saucier version, simply add more olive oil. Try it also with grilled chicken, fish, or veggies.

½   cup loosely packed fresh cilantro leaves
½   cup loosely packed fresh flat-leaf parsley leaves
2   garlic cloves
¼   cup freshly grated Parmesan cheese

2   Tbsp. raw pumpkin seeds, toasted
¼   tsp. salt
¼   cup olive oil

1. Pulse first 6 ingredients in a food processor 10 times or just until chopped. Drizzle olive oil over mixture, and pulse 6 more times or until a coarse mixture forms. Cover and chill up to 24 hours.
Note: To toast pumpkin seeds, see Step 1 of Candied Pumpkin Seeds on page 196.

quick finds From pumpkin seeds to ground spices, head to your favorite **Latin market** to stock up on ingredients for this menu.

Creamy Black Bean-and-Rice Bake

makes 10 servings   hands-on time: 5 min.   **total time: 30 min.**

Expect a spicy kick from the layer of pepper Jack cheese covering the casserole, but if you prefer a milder taste, use Monterey Jack or Cheddar cheese.

1 (8-oz.) package refrigerated prechopped onion	2 (15-oz.) cans seasoned black beans, drained
1 Tbsp. butter	1 (8-oz.) container sour cream
3 (8.5-oz.) pouches ready-to-serve Southwest-flavored whole grain rice medley	1 (4.5-oz.) can chopped green chiles, drained
	1 (8-oz.) block pepper Jack cheese, shredded

1. Preheat oven to 400°. Combine onion and butter in a small microwave-safe bowl; cover tightly with plastic wrap. Microwave at HIGH 3 minutes.

2. Microwave rice according to package directions. Combine onion mixture, rice, and next 3 ingredients. Spoon rice mixture into a lightly greased 13- x 9-inch baking dish; sprinkle with cheese.

3. Bake at 400° for 20 to 23 minutes or until bubbly.

Note: We tested with Uncle Ben's Santa Fe Whole Grain Medley.

Southwestern Salad with Candied Pumpkin Seeds

makes 8 servings   hands-on time: 5 min.   **total time: 30 min.,** including seeds

Use a fork to crumble queso fresco (fresh Mexican cheese), which adds an authentic flavor experience to this salad. If you have trouble locating it, mild feta cheese is a good substitute.

¾ cup Candied Pumpkin Seeds

½ cup olive oil vinaigrette

½ tsp. ground cumin

2 (5-oz.) packages sweet baby greens

1 cup crumbled queso fresco (fresh Mexican cheese, about 4 oz.)

1. Prepare Candied Pumpkin Seeds.

2. Meanwhile, stir together vinaigrette and cumin. Toss greens with dressing, and arrange on a serving platter. Sprinkle with queso fresco and pumpkin seeds. Serve immediately.

candied pumpkin seeds

makes about 4¾ cups   hands-on time: 17 min.   **total time: 25 min.**

Toast seeds in a skillet until puffed, but watch them closely, and don't brown them, or they will taste burned. Find pumpkin seeds (aka *pepitas*) at health food stores, Hispanic markets, and specialty grocery stores.

2 cups raw pumpkin seeds

½ cup granulated sugar

½ cup firmly packed light brown sugar

1 Tbsp. paprika

¾ tsp. salt

3 Tbsp. fresh orange juice

Parchment paper

1. Preheat oven to 350°. Cook pumpkin seeds in a medium-size nonstick skillet over medium heat, stirring often, 8 to 10 minutes or until puffed. (Do not brown.) Transfer to a medium bowl.

2. Combine granulated sugar and next 3 ingredients.

3. Toss pumpkin seeds with orange juice. Add sugar mixture, tossing to coat. Spread in a single layer on a parchment paper-lined jelly-roll pan.

4. Bake at 350° for 6 minutes, stirring once.

Make Ahead Note: Cool in pan on a wire rack 30 minutes. Store in an airtight container up to 2 days.

Trés Leches Trifles with Summer Berries

makes 12 servings   hands-on time: 20 min.   **total time: 20 min.**

This dessert is a delectable cross between summer pudding and trés leches (three milks) cake.

1   qt. fresh strawberries, quartered
1   pt. fresh raspberries
1   pt. fresh blackberries
1   pt. fresh blueberries
½   cup sugar

1   (16-oz.) angel food cake
1   (14-oz.) can sweetened condensed milk
½   cup half-and-half
2   cups whipping cream, whipped

1. Combine first 5 ingredients in a large bowl; toss gently. Let stand 5 minutes.
2. Meanwhile, cut cake into 1-inch cubes. Whisk together condensed milk and half-and-half in a medium bowl.
3. Divide half of cake cubes among 12 (12-oz.) glasses (about 3 to 4 cubes per glass). Top each with 1 Tbsp. milk mixture. Top each with about ¼ cup berry mixture. Divide half of whipped cream among glasses (about ¼ cup each). Repeat layers once.

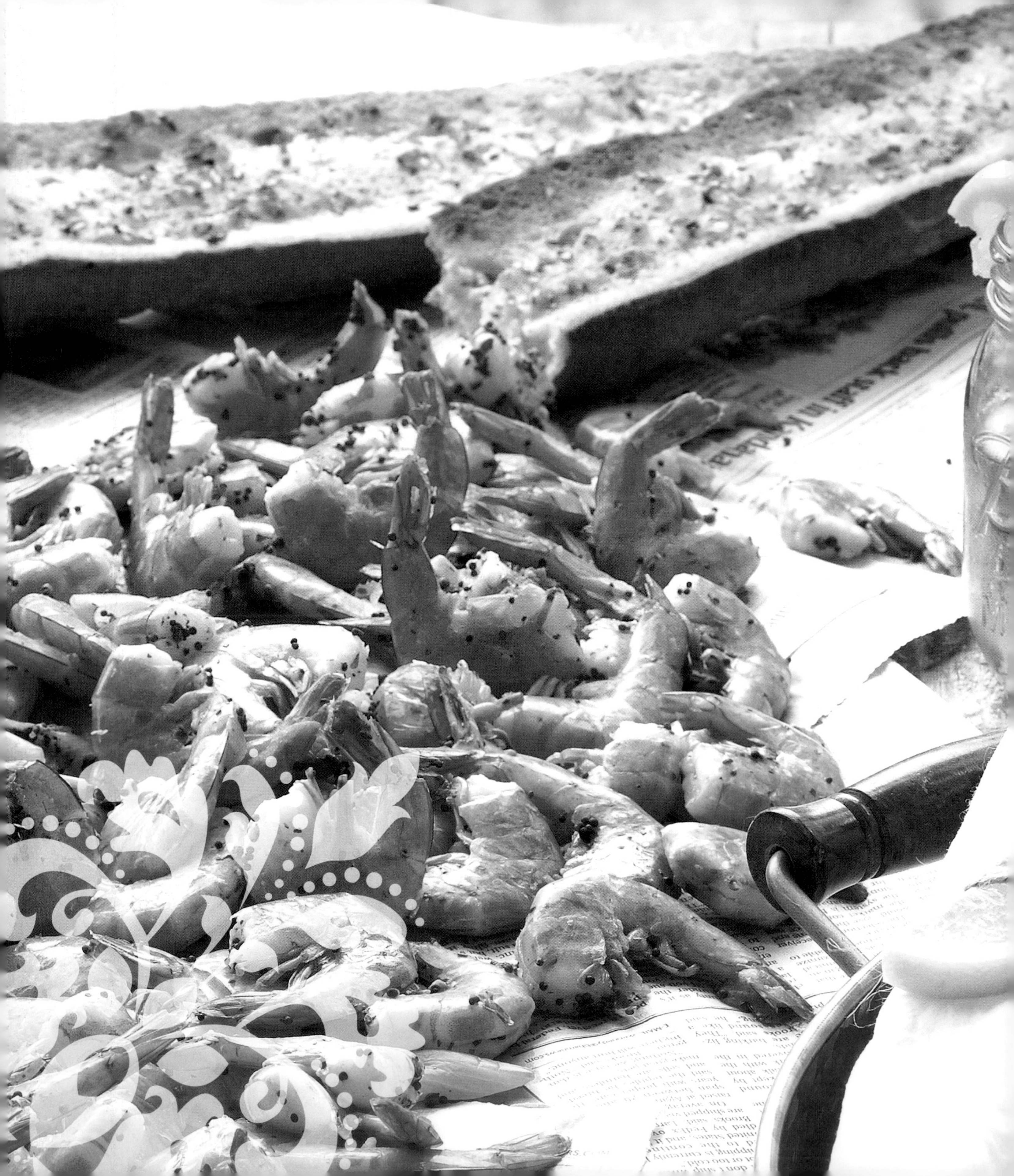

shrimp boil

menu

serves 6 to 8

Boiled Shrimp

Criolla Rémoulade

Timmy's Shrimp Sauce

Spicy Grilled Corn

Garlic-Herb Bread

There is no better way to celebrate summer in the South than with a seafood feast by the shore or in your backyard. Cover the table in newspapers for easy cleanup that can be wrapped and tossed almost as quickly as the menu comes together.

hostess
hit list:

Old and new jars make perfect containers for serving sauces and iced tea. You can purchase a dozen new ones for less than $18 at most supercenters.

The day before:

- Prepare rémoulade sauce; cover and chill
- Prepare Timmy's Shrimp Sauce; cover and chill
- Roll napkins
- Make tags for sauces

30 minutes before:

- Grill corn
- Prepare bread
- Boil shrimp

15 minutes before:

- Cut lemons for shrimp and napkin rolls

Just before serving:

- Sprinkle bread with chives
- Set out sauces

Boiled Shrimp

makes 6 to 8 servings   hands-on time: 5 min.   **total time: 30 min.**

Serve with your favorite cocktail sauce or one of the sauces below.

2   (3-oz.) packages boil-in-bag shrimp-and-crab boil
1   large lemon, halved
1   small onion

3   Tbsp. salt
4   lb. unpeeled, large raw shrimp (21/25 count)
Garnish: lemon wedges

1. Bring first 4 ingredients and 4 qt. water to a boil in a large Dutch oven over high heat. Cover and boil 3 to 4 minutes.

2. Add shrimp; remove from heat. Cover and let stand 10 minutes. (Shrimp will turn pink, and shells will loosen slightly.) Drain, discarding lemon, onion, and boil bags. Garnish, if desired.

Note: We tested with Zatarain's Shrimp & Crab Boil. Some of the seasonings seep out of the bag as the shrimp cook; rinse the shrimp after cooking, if you'd like, or leave the seasonings on for a little extra flavor.

Criolla Rémoulade

makes 1½ cups   hands-on time: 10 min.   **total time: 10 min.**

This is the classic mayonnaise-based rémoulade, spiked with a touch of seafood seasoning.

1   cup mayonnaise
¼   cup Creole mustard
¼   cup chopped sweet pickles
1   Tbsp. minced fresh parsley
2   Tbsp. capers, drained

2   tsp. Worcestershire sauce
2   tsp. horseradish
2   tsp. anchovy paste
1   tsp. Old Bay seasoning
1   tsp. paprika

1. Stir together all ingredients; cover and chill up to 1 week.

Timmy's Shrimp Sauce

makes about 1 cup   hands-on time: 5 min.   **total time: 5 min.**

1   cup mayonnaise
2   Tbsp. ketchup

1   Tbsp. dill pickle relish

1. Stir together all ingredients. Store in an airtight container in refrigerator up to 7 days.

Spicy Grilled Corn

makes 8 servings   hands-on time: 10 min.   **total time: 26 min.**

You can also try the butter sauce with boiled shrimp.

8   ears fresh corn, husks removed
2   Tbsp. olive oil
½   cup butter, melted
2   Tbsp. chopped fresh chives

1   Tbsp. hot sauce
2   tsp. Old Bay seasoning
Lemon wedges

1. Preheat grill to 350° to 400° (medium-high) heat. Rub corn with oil. Grill, covered with grill lid, 16 to 18 minutes or until done, turning every 4 to 5 minutes. (Some kernels will char and pop.)

2. Meanwhile, stir together butter and next 3 ingredients in a bowl. Drizzle 1 Tbsp. butter mixture over each ear of corn. Squeeze juice from lemon wedges over corn. Serve immediately.

Garlic-Herb Bread

makes 8 servings   hands-on time: 10 min.   **total time: 23 min.**

Dried crushed red pepper spices up your usual garlic bread.

3 garlic cloves, minced	½ tsp. dried crushed red pepper
2 Tbsp. extra virgin olive oil	1 (16-oz.) French bread loaf
2 Tbsp. butter, melted	1 Tbsp. chopped fresh chives

1. Preheat oven to 350°. Stir together first 4 ingredients in a small bowl.

2. Cut bread in half lengthwise. Brush cut sides with garlic mixture; place on a baking sheet.

3. Bake at 350° for 13 to 15 minutes or until golden brown. Sprinkle with chives just before serving.

"Keep this get-together super casual. Secure labels
and lemons with garden twine, and serve the food
directly on the newspaper...no dishes required."

kentucky derby

menu

serves 8

Fresh Basil Julep

Derby Cheese Hat

Mini Crab Cakes with Garlic-Chive Sauce

Tomato-Basil Grit Cakes

Fudge-Frosted Brownie Cookies

The Derby is considered "the fastest two minutes in sports," and this party might well be called "the fastest fancy come-together ever!" Bite-size pick-up food is both dainty and divine, and is served up in just 30 minutes with a little advance prep the day before.

hostess
hit list:

Let the run for roses dictate your decor. Think red and roses everywhere. Take this party to the finish line with your prettiest china and silver.

The day before:

- Prepare Basil Simple Syrup; cover and chill
- Prepare Garlic-Chive Sauce; cover and chill
- Make grit cakes; cover and chill
- Make brownie cookies; cover

🕐 30 minutes before:

- Prepare crab cakes

🕐 15 minutes before:

- Assemble cheese hat
- Assemble grit cakes
- Frost cookies to serve

🕐 Just before serving:

- Prepare juleps as guests arrive
- Assemble crab cakes and sauce on platter

Fresh Basil Julep

makes 1 serving   hands-on time: 10 min.   **total time: 20 min.,** not including simple syrup

If you prefer a traditional julep, substitute fresh mint for the basil in the drink recipe and the simple syrup.

3   fresh basil leaves
1   Tbsp. Basil Simple Syrup
Crushed ice
2   Tbsp. (1 oz.) bourbon

1   (4-inch) cocktail straw
1   fresh basil sprig
Powdered sugar (optional)

1. Place basil leaves and Basil Simple Syrup in a julep cup or an 8- to 10-oz. glass. Gently press leaves against sides of cup with back of a spoon to release flavor. Pack cup tightly with crushed ice; pour bourbon over ice. Insert straw, and place basil sprig directly next to straw. Sprinkle with powdered sugar, if desired.
Note: We tested with Woodford Reserve Distiller's Select bourbon.

basil simple syrup

makes 1½ cups   hands-on time: 10 min.   **total time: 10 min.,** not including cooling and chilling

1 cup sugar   1 cup firmly packed fresh basil leaves

1. Bring 1 cup sugar and 1 cup water to a boil in a medium saucepan. Boil, stirring often, 1 minute or until sugar is dissolved. Remove from heat; add basil leaves, and cool completely (about 1 hour). Pour into a glass jar. Cover and chill 24 hours. Remove and discard basil.

Derby Cheese Hat

makes 12 servings   hands-on time: 10 min.   **total time: 10 min.**

1   (13.2-oz., 5¼-inch) Brie round
1   (5.2-oz., 2¾-inch) buttery garlic-and-herb
     spreadable cheese round

Garnishes: ribbon; herb bouquet of fresh lavender, fresh
          thyme sprigs, and fresh mint sprigs
Assorted crackers

1. Place Brie round on a serving platter. Top with spreadable cheese round. Garnish, if desired. Serve with assorted crackers.
Note: We tested with Boursin spreadable cheese.

Mini Crab Cakes

makes 16 cakes   hands-on time: 15 min.   **total time: 30 min.,** not including sauce

1   (8-oz.) package fresh lump crabmeat, drained
3   whole grain white bread slices
⅓   cup light mayonnaise
3   green onions, thinly sliced
1   tsp. Old Bay seasoning
1   tsp. Worcestershire sauce

2   large eggs, lightly beaten
Vegetable cooking spray
Salt to taste
Garlic-Chive Sauce
Garnish: chopped fresh chives

1. Pick crabmeat, removing any bits of shell. Pulse bread slices in a blender or food processor 5 times or until finely crumbled. (Yield should be about 1½ cups.)

2. Stir together mayonnaise and next 4 ingredients in a large bowl. Gently stir in breadcrumbs and crabmeat. Shape mixture into 16 (2-inch) cakes (about 2 Tbsp. each).

3. Cook cakes, in batches, on a hot, large griddle or nonstick skillet coated with cooking spray over medium-low heat 4 minutes on each side or until golden brown. Season with salt to taste. (Keep cakes warm in a 200° oven for up to 30 minutes.) Serve with Garlic-Chive Sauce and garnish, if desired.

Note: We tested with Sara Lee Soft & Smooth Whole Grain White Bread.

garlic-chive sauce

makes about 1 cup   hands-on time: 10 min.   **total time: 30 min.**

¾   cup light sour cream*
1   garlic clove, minced
1   Tbsp. chopped fresh chives
¾   tsp. lemon zest

1½ Tbsp. fresh lemon juice
¼   tsp. salt
⅛   tsp. pepper

1. Stir together all ingredients in a small bowl. Cover and chill 20 minutes before serving.

*Light mayonnaise may be substituted.

quick finds Inexpensive **plastic julep cups** can be found at **flower wholesalers.** Put them to use as vases. Serve the cocktail in the real deal.

Tomato-Basil Grit Cakes

makes about 50 mini-cakes   hands-on time: 18 min.   **total time: 23 min.**

1¼ cup uncooked quick-cooking grits
½ tsp. salt
¼ cup (1 oz.) shredded Parmesan cheese
¼ tsp. garlic powder

¼ tsp. pepper
½ cup jarred pesto
2 plum tomatoes, diced
Garnish: small basil leaves

1. Combine 3 cups water, grits, and salt in a medium-size, heavy saucepan; bring to a boil, stirring constantly. Reduce heat; simmer, covered, 5 minutes or until grits are very thick, stirring often. Remove grits from heat, and stir in Parmesan cheese, garlic powder, and pepper; pour onto baking sheet. Spread into a 10-inch square (about ⅜-inch thick); freeze 5 minutes.

2. Cut into 25 (2- x 2-inch) squares. Cut each square in half diagonally. Top with pesto and diced tomatoes. Garnish, if desired.

Fudge-Frosted Brownie Cookies

makes 20 cookies   hands-on time: 5 min.   **total time: 26 min.**

Stack and bake store-bought refrigerated cookie and brownie dough, and then smother with a delectable homemade frosting for an easy, unexpected treat.

½ (16-oz.) package refrigerated chocolate chip cookie dough squares

½ (16-oz.) package refrigerated miniature brownie dough bites

½ cup butter

⅓ cup milk

¼ cup unsweetened cocoa

3 cups powdered sugar

½ tsp. vanilla extract

1 cup chopped walnuts

1. Preheat oven to 350°. Place one cookie dough square in each cup of 2 lightly greased (12-cup) muffin pans, filling 20 cups. Top each with a brownie bite, pressing together gently.

2. Bake at 350° for 16 to 18 minutes or until done.

3. Combine butter and next 2 ingredients in a saucepan; cook over medium heat, stirring often, 5 minutes or until butter melts. Remove from heat; beat in powdered sugar and vanilla at low speed with an electric mixer just until blended. Stir in walnuts.

4. Spoon frosting over warm cookies. Serve warm or at room temperature.

Note: We tested with Nestle Toll House Refrigerated Chocolate Chip Cookie Dough and Refrigerated Miniature Brownie Dough Bites.

fondue fun

menu

serves 6

Two-Cheese-and-Honey Fondue

Tomato-and-Herb Fondue

Mesclun Salad in Minutes

Mississippi Mud Fondue

sparkling wine with fresh raspberries

What's old is new again, and fondue parties are all the rage. This menu boasts a lighter, tomato-based sauce served alongside a more traditional cheese fondue for balance. Cap the meal with a decadent dessert sauce for dipping.

hostess
hit list:

The key to the success of this party is keeping things warm. If you don't have fondue pots, you can use hot plates, chafing dishes, or slow cookers.

The day before:

- Prepare accompaniments for Tomato-and-Herb Fondue and Mississippi Mud Fondue
- Prepare Tomato-and-Herb Fondue; cover and chill
- Shred cheeses for fondue; seal in zip-top plastic bags

🕐 30 minutes before:

- Prepare Two-Cheese-and-Honey Fondue and keep warm
- Prepare Mississippi Mud Fondue; keep warm
- Reheat Tomato-and-Herb Fondue; keep warm

🕐 15 minutes before:

- Prepare the salad

🕐 Just before serving:

- Set up all fondue trays of accompaniments

Two-Cheese-and-Honey Fondue

makes 2¼ cups   hands-on time: 23 min.   **total time: 23 min.**

Fondue:

1   cup heavy cream
1   cup chicken broth
1   Tbsp. honey
2   cups (8 oz.) freshly shredded
     Jarlsberg cheese

½   cup (2 oz.) freshly shredded Swiss cheese
¼   cup all-purpose flour
¼   tsp. dry mustard
¼   tsp. cracked pepper

Serve with:

Cubed ciabatta bread, sliced pears, sliced apples

1. Bring heavy cream, chicken broth, and honey to a boil over medium-high heat in a 3-qt. saucepan; reduce heat to medium-low, and simmer.

2. Meanwhile, combine cheeses and next 3 ingredients in a large bowl. Slowly whisk cheese mixture into simmering broth mixture until melted and smooth. Transfer to a fondue pot; keep warm. Serve with desired accompaniments.

Tomato-and-Herb Fondue

makes 3 cups   hands-on time: 21 min.   **total time: 21 min.**

Fondue:

1   Tbsp. butter
¼   cup chopped sweet onion
2   garlic cloves, minced
2   (14.5-oz.) cans fire-roasted diced tomatoes
1   tsp. tomato paste

½   tsp. lemon zest
¼   cup chopped fresh basil

Serve with:

Cubed, lightly toasted French bread; cubed, toasted cheese bread; chopped, cooked chicken tenders; meatballs; tortellini

1. Melt butter in a large saucepan over medium heat; add onion and garlic, and sauté 3 minutes or until vegetables are tender.

2. Add tomatoes, tomato paste, and lemon zest, and cook, stirring occasionally, 8 to 10 minutes. Remove from heat, and stir in basil. Transfer to a fondue pot; keep warm. Serve with desired accompaniments.

> **"**If you have enameled cast iron, this is a good time to use it. It retains heat longer than other types of pans.**"**

Mesclun Salad in Minutes

makes 6 servings   hands-on time: 5 min.   **total time: 5 min.**

1   (5-oz.) package baby lettuces
½   pt. grape tomatoes, halved
½   cup extra virgin olive oil
¼   cup balsamic vinegar

1   tsp. coarse-grained Dijon mustard
½   tsp. kosher salt
¼   tsp. freshly ground pepper

1. Toss together first 2 ingredients in a salad bowl.

2. Place remaining ingredients in a jar with a tight-fitting lid. Shake vigorously 30 seconds. Pour over salad, and toss to coat. Serve immediately.

Mississippi Mud Fondue

makes 4 cups   hands-on time: 18 min.   **total time: 18 min.**

Fondue:

1   cup heavy cream
1   (12-oz.) package dark chocolate morsels
1   (7½-oz.) jar marshmallow crème
½   tsp. vanilla extract

Serve with:

Brownies, biscotti, graham crackers, marshmallows, chopped toasted pecans, chopped candied ginger

1. Bring cream to a boil in a large heavy saucepan over medium-high heat; reduce heat to low, and simmer. Add chocolate morsels, and stir until melted and smooth. Stir in marshmallow crème and vanilla, stirring constantly until smooth. Transfer to a fondue pot; keep warm. Serve with desired accompaniments.

quick finds **Long bamboo skewers** are great stand-ins for fondue forks. Plus, you can toss them rather than wash them after the party.

book club supper

menu

---

serves 6 to 8

Blackberry Cocktail

Melon, Mozzarella, and Prosciutto Skewers

Spinach-Tortellini Soup

Chocolate-Hazelnut Tartlets

An informal get-together deserves a laid-back menu to match. Toss a few oversized pillows on the floor, and cozy up to the coffee table to discuss the most recent pick.

hostess
hit list:

A hearty soup is always an easy item to pull together quickly, and it's ideal for a casual gathering. If you don't have enough soup bowls, improvise and fill in with mugs or other pieces that can handle the heat.

The day before:

- Prepare the skewers without pepper; chill
- Bake tart shells; store in refrigerator in airtight container
- Slice cucumbers and juice limes for cocktail; chill

30 minutes before:

- Prepare cocktail
- Prepare soup

15 minutes before:

- Pipe shells with hazelnut filling, and garnish

Just before serving:

- Sprinkle skewers with pepper

Blackberry Cocktail

makes 5 cups   hands-on time: 20 min.   **total time: 20 min.**

1   (0.75-oz.) package fresh mint sprigs
12 (¼-inch-thick) cucumber slices
2   (6-oz.) packages fresh blackberries
¾   cup fresh lime juice (about 3 limes)
8 to 12 tsp. turbinado sugar*

1   cup plus 2 Tbsp. gin
1   cup cold club soda
Crushed ice
Garnishes: cucumber slices, fresh blackberries, lime
      wedges, lemon mint sprigs

1. Place first 5 ingredients in a large pitcher. Gently press mint leaves, cucumbers, and blackberries against side of pitcher with a wooden spoon to release flavors. Stir in gin and club soda. Serve over ice. Garnish, if desired.

*Superfine or powdered sugar may be substituted.

Melon, Mozzarella, and Prosciutto Skewers

makes 20 skewers   hands-on time: 20 min.   **total time: 20 min.**

Put out half of the skewers, and keep the remaining chilled until ready to replenish.

20 (1-inch) cantaloupe or honeydew cubes (about
      2½ cups)
20 thin slices prosciutto (about ½ lb.)
20 fresh small mozzarella cheese balls (about
      1 [8-oz.] tub)

20 (4-inch) wooden skewers
Freshly cracked pepper

1. Thread 1 melon cube, 1 prosciutto slice, and 1 mozzarella ball onto each wooden skewer. Sprinkle with cracked pepper just before serving.
Note: We tested with Il Villaggio Mozzarella Fior di Latte Ciliegine cheese.

hostess helper Pressed for time? Arrange pre-cut, purchased **melon balls, mozzarella balls,** and thin strips of **prosciutto** on a pretty platter. Serve with **toothpicks** on the side.

Spinach-Tortellini Soup

makes 16 cups   hands-on time: 10 min.   total time: 30 min.

1   (14-oz.) can chicken broth

2   extra-large vegetable bouillon cubes

1   (10-oz.) package frozen chopped spinach

2   (14½-oz.) cans stewed tomatoes

1   garlic clove, minced

2   (9-oz.) packages refrigerated cheese-filled tortellini

½   cup (2 oz.) shredded Parmesan cheese

1. Bring broth, bouillon cubes, and 4 cups water to a boil in a Dutch oven over medium-high heat.

2. Add spinach, stewed tomatoes, and garlic, and return mixture to a boil.

3. Stir in tortellini, and cook 5 minutes. Sprinkle each serving with shredded Parmesan cheese.

Note: We tested with Knorr Vegetable Bouillon Cubes.

hip tip Mail out laminated bookmark **invitations** to your book club friends for a fitting and useful reminder of the **date** of the gathering, the **book** you'll be discussing, and even what's on the **menu.**

Chocolate-Hazelnut Tartlets

makes 6 to 8 appetizer servings   hands-on time: 15 min.   **total time: 15 min.,** not including shells

½ cup jarred hazelnut spread
24 Flaky Tartlet Shells

Garnishes: sweetened whipped cream, roasted salted hazelnuts

1. Spoon hazelnut spread into a 1-qt. heavy-duty zip-top plastic bag (do not seal). Snip 1 corner of bag to make a small hole. Pipe hazelnut spread into Flaky Tartlet Shells. Garnish, if desired.
Note: We tested with Nutella Hazelnut Spread.

flaky tartlet shells

makes 24 tartlet shells   hands-on time: 15 min.   **total time: 21 min.**

If you are making several batches of shells, you can stack up to three unrolled piecrusts on top of each other and cut dough circles all at once. A tart tamper or drink muddler makes fast work of pressing dough into pans. (Both are available at kitchenware stores.)

½ (14.1-oz.) package refrigerated piecrust

1. Preheat oven to 425°. Unroll piecrust on a flat surface. Cut into 24 rounds using a 2-inch round cutter. Press rounds onto bottoms of an ungreased 24-cup miniature muffin pan. (Dough will come slightly up sides, forming a cup.) Prick bottom of each dough circle 4 times with a fork.
2. Bake at 425° for 6 to 8 minutes or until golden. Remove from pans to a wire rack, and let cool before filling.
Make Ahead: Store baked tartlet shells in an airtight container in refrigerator up to 2 days, or freeze up to 1 month. Thaw at room temperature 2 hours before filling.

tailgate party

menu

serves 6

Spicy Bloody Mary Pitcher

Simple Grits Bar

Southwestern Pigs in a Blanket

Mini Churros or bakery cinnamon rolls

This crowd-pleasing brunch menu is perfect for kicking off a day filled with football games to watch on television. Be sure to show your team spirit from plates to platters. Ribbons and school pins make fun accents and can be found at school bookstores, hobby shops, and flea markets.

hostess
hit list:

Layering folded and pressed fabric in team colors creates an effortless table covering. Accent with neutral linens and silverware to balance the look.

The day before:

- Gather serving pieces
- Tie utensils with ribbon in team colors
- Secure ribbons with team logo pins
- Prepare and chill grits toppings, covered, in serving bowls
- Stir together beverage in serving pitcher, omitting vodka and garnish; cover and chill

 ### 30 minutes before:

- Assemble and bake pigs in a blanket
- Make Mini Churros

15 minutes before:

- Cook Simple Grits

Just before serving:

- Add vodka to beverage, and arrange garnishes on a serving tray around pitcher

Spicy Bloody Mary Pitcher

makes 6 servings   hands-on time: 5 min.   **total time: 5 min.**

1   (32-oz.) bottle spicy Bloody Mary mix
1   cup vodka
¼   cup fresh lime juice
1   Tbsp. Worcestershire sauce

1   tsp. celery salt
Garnishes: celery sticks, pickled okra, lemon and lime
      wedges

1. Stir together Bloody Mary mix and remaining ingredients. Serve over ice. Garnish, if desired.
Note: We tested with Zing Zang Bloody Mary Mix.

Simple Grits Bar

makes 8 servings   hands-on time: 5 min.   **total time: 18 min.**

Let guests customize their grits by offering an array of toppings.

2   tsp. salt
2   cups uncooked quick-cooking grits
6   Tbsp. butter
½   tsp. pepper

Toppings: hot sauce, sliced green onions, chopped
      tomatoes, cooked and crumbled bacon, peeled and
      cooked shrimp, shredded Gouda cheese, shredded
      Cheddar cheese

1. Bring salt and 8 cups water to a boil in a Dutch oven over medium-high heat.
2. Whisk in grits, reduce heat to low, and cook, stirring occasionally, 8 minutes or until creamy.
3. Whisk in butter and pepper. Transfer to a slow cooker to keep warm, and serve with desired toppings.

Southwestern Pigs in a Blanket

makes 8 to 10 servings   hands-on time: 5 min.   **total time: 17 min.**

2   (8-oz.) cans refrigerated crescent rolls
1   (8-oz.) package pepper Jack cheese*

2   (9.6-oz.) packages breakfast sausage links
Salsa

1. Preheat oven to 375°. Divide crescent rolls into individual triangles. Cut 4 pepper Jack cheese slices each into 4 pieces. Place 1 pepper Jack cheese piece and 1 fully cooked breakfast sausage link in center of each dough triangle. Roll up, starting at wide end. Arrange on an ungreased baking sheet.
2. Bake at 375° for 12 minutes or until golden brown. Serve with salsa.
*Cheddar cheese may be substituted.
Note: We tested with Jimmy Dean Fully Cooked Original Pork Sausage Links.

Mini Churros

makes 15 churros   hands-on time: 20 min.
total time: 23 min.

Vegetable oil

¼ cup sugar

¾ tsp. ground cinnamon

½ cup self-rising flour

1½ Tbsp. sugar

1½ Tbsp. butter

½ tsp. vanilla extract

1 large egg

1. Pour oil to depth of 3 inches into a Dutch oven.
Heat to 360°.
2. Meanwhile, whisk together ¼ cup sugar and ½
tsp. cinnamon in a shallow bowl. Combine flour and
remaining ¼ tsp. cinnamon in a bowl.
3. Place ½ cup water, 1½ Tbsp. sugar, and butter in
a medium saucepan. Bring to a boil; remove from
heat, and add flour mixture, all at once, stirring
vigorously until mixture leaves sides of pan and
forms a ball. Let stand 1 minute. Add vanilla and
egg, beating vigorously with a wooden spoon until
smooth.
4. Spoon batter into a pastry bag fitted with a ⅜-
inch star tip. Carefully pipe batter, 5 (3- to 4-inch-
long) strips at a time, into hot oil. (Use a paring knife
to release strips of batter from pastry tip.) Fry 1 to 2
minutes on each side or until browned; drain on
paper towels. Roll hot churros in cinnamon-sugar
mixture. Serve warm or at room temperature.

kidding
around

Entertaining the little ones is easy when you follow these fun party ideas full of whimsy, and they're designed to elicit smiles from kids of all ages.

doggy birthday party

menu

---

serves 8

Extra Cheesy Grilled Cheese

tortilla chips

juice boxes

Milk Chocolate-Peanut Butter Mini Cupcakes

Fido's Peanut Butter Pupcakes

Okay, it's true. In the South we love a good party. Sometimes we kick up our heels for no reason at all. If you are one of those who needs a reason, why not celebrate man's best friend? Whether it's Fido's birthday or the anniversary of the day he joined the family, it is certainly an honorable cause worthy of celebration. So tell your friends to bring their pups and come sit...stay...and play awhile.

hostess
hit list:

The proof is in the pupcakes. Pooches will be smitten with dog-friendly confections all their own. Sing "Happy Birthday," let them eat cake, and then send them to the yard to play while you and your guests catch-up.

The day before:

- Bake and frost mini cupcakes; store in airtight container in refrigerator
- Bake and frost pupcakes; store in airtight container in refrigerator
- Prepare treat bags

30 minutes before:

- Prepare grilled cheese
- Set juice boxes in iced containers

Just before serving:

- Garnish pupcakes with dog treats

Extra Cheesy Grilled Cheese

makes 8 servings   hands-on time: 30 min.   **total time: 30 min.**

½   cup butter, softened

2   Tbsp. grated Parmesan cheese

16   Italian bread slices

Wax paper

8   (¾-oz.) provolone cheese slices

8   (¾-oz.) mozzarella cheese slices

1. Stir together butter and Parmesan cheese in a small bowl.

2. Spread 1½ tsp. butter mixture on 1 side of each bread slice. Place 8 bread slices, buttered sides down, on wax paper. Top with provolone and mozzarella cheeses; top with remaining bread slices, buttered sides up.

3. Cook sandwiches, in 2 batches, on a large hot griddle or in a nonstick skillet over medium heat, gently pressing with a spatula, 4 minutes on each side or until golden brown and cheese is melted.

hostess helper Serve the food on festive **paper plates** for easy cleanup, and take the party outside.

Milk Chocolate-Peanut Butter Mini Cupcakes

makes 20 cupcakes   hands-on time: 12 min.   **total time: 30 min.**

Look for miniature paper baking cups with flair for these bite-size treats.

Cupcakes

¼ cup milk chocolate morsels
¼ cup butter, softened
¼ cup granulated sugar
2 Tbsp. brown sugar
1 large egg
½ cup all-purpose flour
2 Tbsp. unsweetened cocoa
¼ tsp. baking powder
⅛ tsp. salt
¼ cup buttermilk

½ tsp. vanilla extract
20 miniature paper baking cups

Peanut Butter Frosting

½ cup creamy peanut butter
¼ cup butter, softened
1 cup powdered sugar
1 Tbsp. heavy cream
¼ tsp. vanilla extract

Garnish

Chocolate candy sprinkles

1. Prepare cupcakes: Preheat oven to 375°. Microwave chocolate morsels in a microwave-safe bowl at HIGH 1 minute or until melted, stirring at 30-second intervals.

2. Beat butter and sugars at medium speed with an electric mixer until fluffy. Add egg, beating just until blended.

3. Combine flour and next 3 ingredients; add to butter mixture alternately with buttermilk, beginning and ending with flour mixture. Beat at low speed just until blended after each addition. Stir in melted chocolate morsels and vanilla.

4. Place mini baking cups in a 24-cup miniature muffin pan. Spoon batter into cups, filling two-thirds full.

5. Bake at 375° for 14 minutes or until a wooden pick inserted in center comes out clean. Remove from pans to wire racks; place cupcakes in freezer 4 minutes.

6. Meanwhile, prepare Peanut Butter Frosting: Beat peanut butter and butter at medium speed with an electric mixer until creamy. Gradually add sugar, beating until smooth. Add heavy cream and vanilla, beating just until blended. Spread frosting on tops of cupcakes. Garnish, if desired. Store in an airtight container in refrigerator up to 2 days.

Note: For a more decorative look, pipe the frosting. Insert metal tip no. 4B (large star tip) into a large decorating bag; fill with frosting. Pipe frosting onto cupcakes.

"An apothecary jar filled with dog biscuits provides easy access to treats during the party. Send guests home with doggie bags filled with toy favors."

Fido's Peanut Butter Pupcakes

makes 1 dozen   hands-on time: 5 min.   **total time: 30 min.**

Place baked cakes in the freezer to chill rapidly before icing. While these are safe for people to eat, they are not as tasty for humans as they are for dogs.

Peanut Butter Pupcakes

3   cups whole wheat flour

2   tsp. baking powder

¼   cup unsweetened applesauce

¼   cup creamy peanut butter

2   Tbsp. honey

1   tsp. vanilla extract

12 paper baking cups

Cream Cheese Frosting

1   (8-oz.) package ⅓-less-fat cream cheese

1   Tbsp. all-purpose flour

2   Tbsp. honey

Remaining Ingredients

12 small dog biscuits

1. Prepare Peanut Butter Pupcakes: Preheat oven to 375°. Whisk together flour and baking powder in a large bowl. Combine 2 cups water, applesauce, and next 3 ingredients; add to flour mixture. Beat at medium speed with an electric mixer just until blended.

2. Place baking cups in a 12-cup muffin pan. Spoon batter into cups, filling three-fourths full.

3. Bake at 375° for 17 minutes or until cakes spring back when touched. Remove from pans to a wire rack; place in freezer 8 to 10 minutes or until completely cool.

3. Meanwhile, prepare Cream Cheese Frosting: Beat cream cheese with an electric mixer until fluffy. Add flour and honey, beating until smooth. Spread frosting on tops of pupcakes, and top each with a dog biscuit. Store in airtight container in refrigerator up to 2 days.

Note: We tested with Milk-Bone Small Dog Biscuits.

family game night

menu

serves 8

Hot Pimiento Cheese-Bacon Dip

Tropical Fruit Kabobs with Coconut Dip

Mini Cheeseburger Pizzas

S'Mores 'n' More Snack Mix

Turn off the TV, switch off your cell phones, and power down the computer. Gather around a game board, and share some quality time together as a family. With unplugged fun and a menu to please even the most finicky, you might be surprised to find out your kids would rather be home together than anywhere else.

hostess
hit list:

While we pull out all the stops when we entertain friends, we often don't push the envelope with family at home. Kids will delight in these classic favorites served with party panache.

The day before:

- Cut pineapple and kiwifruit for the kabobs; cover and chill
- Prepare snack mix; cover and store in an airtight container
- Prepare celery for Hot Pimiento Cheese-Bacon Dip; cover and chill

30 minutes before:

- Prepare Coconut Dip; cover and chill
- Assemble pizzas

15 minutes before:

- Prepare Hot Pimiento Cheese-Bacon Dip
- Slice bananas, and assemble fruit kabobs. Set out Coconut Dip
- Bake pizzas

Just before serving:

- Set out the games

"Family-friendly cheese dip doesn't get any easier than this dressed-up pimiento cheese. Slice and use whatever raw veggies you have on hand as dippers."

Hot Pimiento Cheese-Bacon Dip

makes 2½ cups   hands-on time: 8 min.   **total time: 8 min.**

1   (12-oz.) container jalapeño pimiento cheese
1   (8-oz.) package cream cheese, softened
⅛   tsp. garlic powder

6   fully-cooked bacon slices
Celery sticks
Bagel chips

1. Microwave first 2 ingredients in a medium-size, microwave-safe bowl at HIGH 1½ minutes or until cheeses are soft, stirring after 1 minute. Stir in garlic powder.

2. Heat bacon according to package directions. Crumble bacon; sprinkle over hot dip. Serve with celery sticks and bagel chips.

Note: We tested with Palmetto Cheese Gourmet Spread with Jalapeños. It's flecked with jalapeño pepper bits. Substitute your favorite pimiento cheese, and stir in 1 to 2 Tbsp. minced fresh jalapeño pepper, if desired.

Tropical Fruit Kabobs with Coconut Dip

makes 8 servings   hands-on time: 15 min.   **total time: 15 min.**

Fruit Skewers, page 259, can be substituted for these fresh fruit sticks.

1   fresh pineapple, peeled and cored
2   bananas
2   kiwifruit, peeled and sliced into 1-inch pieces
8   (8-inch) wooden skewers

½   (8-oz.) package cream cheese, softened
½   cup cream of coconut
1   cup thawed, frozen whipped topping
¼   cup sweetened shredded coconut, toasted (optional)

1. Position pineapple upright on a cutting board. Cut pineapple lengthwise into eighths. Cut half of slices into 1-inch pieces. Reserve remaining pineapple for another use. Slice bananas into 1-inch-thick pieces. Thread pineapple, bananas, and kiwifruit alternately onto skewers.

2. Beat cream cheese at medium speed with an electric mixer until smooth. Gradually add cream of coconut, beating until smooth. Fold in whipped topping. Top with toasted coconut, if desired, and serve with fruit skewers.

Mini Cheeseburger Pizzas

makes 8 servings   hands-on time: 18 min.   **total time: 28 min.**

Depending on your pizza crust preference (thin and crispy or thick and chewy), you can vary your bread base for this snacking pizza. We recommend French rolls that resemble a cross between a hamburger bun and French bread. English muffins and bagels are good options, too.

½ cup ketchup
2 Tbsp. yellow mustard
1 lb. ground round
½ cup refrigerated prechopped onion

2 Tbsp. chopped dill pickle
8 (1-oz.) French bread rolls, split
1 medium tomato, chopped
½ (16-oz.) block American cheese, shredded

1. Preheat oven to 400°. Combine ketchup and mustard.
2. Brown ground beef and onion in a large skillet over medium-high heat, stirring often, 8 minutes or until meat crumbles and is no longer pink; drain. Stir in pickle and 2 Tbsp. ketchup mixture.
3. Place rolls, cut sides up, on a large lightly greased baking sheet. Spread remaining ketchup mixture on rolls. Top with beef mixture and chopped tomato; sprinkle with cheese.
4. Bake at 400° for 10 minutes or until cheese melts and rolls are toasted.

S'mores 'n' More Snack Mix

makes 24 servings   hands-on time: 10 min.   **total time: 30 min.**

7 cups honey graham cereal
2 cups honey-roasted peanuts
½ cup butter
1 cup firmly packed brown sugar

¼ cup light corn syrup
1½ cups miniature marshmallows
1 cup semisweet chocolate morsels or candy-coated chocolate pieces

1. Preheat oven to 325°. Combine cereal and peanuts in a very large bowl.
2. Melt butter in a saucepan over medium-low heat; add sugar and corn syrup. Bring to a boil over medium heat; boil 2 minutes.
3. Pour butter mixture over cereal mixture, stirring to coat. Spread in a single layer on a lightly greased aluminum foil-lined jelly-roll pan.
4. Bake at 325° for 10 minutes, stirring after 5 minutes. Let cool completely (about 10 minutes); stir. Toss together cereal mixture, marshmallows, and chocolate morsels in a large bowl. Store in an airtight container up to 5 days.
Note: We tested with Golden Grahams cereal.

S'mores 'n' More
Snack Mix

pool party

menu

serves 8

Watermelon Cooler

Brown Sugar Fruit Dip

Fried Pickles

Mini Ballpark Dogs

Frozen S'mores Bombs

Take the party poolside, and serve these scaled-down, kid-friendly favorites. Add a punch of color to this warm-weather gathering by using unbreakable plastic and paper products in tropical hues.

hostess
hit list:

Hit discount stores for colorful straws, acrylic cups, and beach balls and towels in matching colors.

The day before:

- Set out water toys
- Prepare and freeze Frozen S'mores Bombs
- Make Brown Sugar Fruit Dip; cover and chill
- Cut fruit for Brown Sugar Fruit Dip; cover and chill

30 minutes before:

- Prepare batter and heat oil for pickles
- Prepare Mini Ballpark Dogs

15 minutes before:

- Dip and fry the pickles
- Bake Mini Ballpark Dogs

Just before serving:

- Prepare the Watermelon Cooler
- Set out dip and fruit

Watermelon Cooler

makes about 8 cups   hands-on time: 6 min.   **total time: 6 min.**

6   cups (1-inch) seeded watermelon cubes

1 ½ cups ginger ale

1 ½ cups ice

1   (6-oz.) can frozen limeade concentrate

1. Process half each of watermelon and remaining ingredients in a blender until smooth; pour mixture into a pitcher. Repeat procedure with remaining half of ingredients; pour into pitcher, and serve immediately.

Brown Sugar Fruit Dip

makes about 3½ cups   hands-on time: 10 min.   **total time: 10 min.**

Choose any fresh, seasonal fruit to pair with this creamy dip. We prefer strawberries, pineapple, and grapes.

½   cup firmly packed brown sugar

1   (8-oz.) package cream cheese, softened

1   cup sour cream

1   tsp. vanilla extract

1   cup thawed, frozen whipped topping

Assorted fruit

1. Beat brown sugar and cream cheese at medium speed with an electric mixer until smooth. Add sour cream and vanilla, beating until blended and smooth; fold in whipped topping. Cover and chill until ready to serve. Serve with assorted fruit.

hip tip Hose down the **pool surround** from time to time so that little feet don't get burned.

> **"**Float life preservers in bright colors in the pool for pops of color and added safety.**"**

Fried Pickles

makes 6 to 8 servings   hands-on time: 21 min.   **total time: 21 min.**

1 (16-oz.) jar dill pickle sandwich slices, drained
1 egg white
¾ cup club soda
1½ tsp. baking powder

¼ tsp. seasoned salt
¾ cup all-purpose flour
Vegetable oil
Ranch dressing (optional)

1. Pat pickles dry with paper towels. Slice pickles horizontally in half.

2. Whisk together egg white and next 3 ingredients in a large bowl; add flour, and whisk until smooth.

3. Pour oil to depth of 1½ inches into a large, heavy skillet or Dutch oven; heat over medium-high heat to 375°.

4. Dip pickle slices into batter, allowing excess batter to drip off. Fry pickles, in batches, 3 to 4 minutes or until golden. Drain and pat dry on paper towels. Serve immediately with Ranch dressing for dipping, if desired.

Note: We tested with Vlasic Kosher Dill Stackers.

Mini Ballpark Dogs

makes 12 servings   hands-on time: 15 min.   **total time: 30 min.**

Serve these sloppy Joe-like dogs with plenty of napkins.

24 cocktail-size beef franks
1 (15-oz.) package chili without beans
12 bakery-style dinner rolls, cut in half vertically

2 cups (8 oz.) shredded Cheddar cheese
½ cup dill pickle relish (optional)

1. Preheat oven to 350°. Bring 2 cups water to a light boil in a 3-qt. saucepan over medium-high heat. Add franks, reduce heat to medium-low, and simmer 4 minutes. Drain and keep warm.

2. Microwave chili according to package directions.

3. Meanwhile, cut a slit in each roll half, cutting to but not through bottoms of rolls.

4. Place one frank in each roll, and place in a 13- x 9-inch baking dish. Top each with chili and cheese.

5. Bake at 350° for 8 minutes or until thoroughly heated and cheese melts. Top with relish, if desired.

Note: We tested with Hillshire Farms Lit'l Beef Franks and Hormel No Beans Chili.

Frozen S'mores Bombs

makes 12 servings   hands-on time: 8 min.   **total time: 30 min.**

Pull these treats out of the freezer just before serving. We enjoyed them frozen as well as slightly thawed.

12 wooden picks
12 marshmallows
½ cup milk chocolate morsels
1 tsp shortening

½ cup graham cracker crumbs or other finely crumbled cookie crumbs
⅔ cup toffee bits
Wax paper

1. Insert pointed end of each wooden pick into flat side of each marshmallow.

2. Combine morsels and shortening in a small microwave-safe glass bowl. Microwave at HIGH 1 minute or until melted; stir until smooth. Dip marshmallows into melted chocolate, coating sides and bottoms completely. Quickly dip bottom of each marshmallow in cracker crumbs; roll sides in toffee bits.

3. Place coated marshmallows on a wax paper-lined jelly-roll pan; freeze 20 minutes. Drizzle with any remaining melted chocolate, if desired. Freeze until ready to serve. Store in freezer in a zip-top plastic freezer bag up to 1 week.

fast flourish Think **hands on**...kids delight in foods to dip, treats on a stick, and miniature ballpark favorites.

halloween party

menu

serves 12

Pumpkin Cheese Ball

Mummy Dogs

Harvest Moon Lollipops

vegetable sticks (crudités)

crackers

soft drinks

Set up a harvest table on the front lawn, and invite your neighbors to stop by for a nibble or two before trick-or-treating. Little ghosts and goblins are sure to enjoy a cheese ball disguised as a pumpkin, hot dogs wrapped like mummies, and giant lollipops that are bound to send them over the moon with delight.

hostess
hit list:

For this outside gathering, it's hard to compete with the natural decor of autumn leaves. Add to it with a few pumpkins, flickering candles, and bales of hay for seating and serving.

The day before:

- Make Pumpkin Cheese Ball without stem, vine, or leaf; cover and chill
- Make lollipops; lay on wax paper
- Slice vegetables for Pumpkin Cheese Ball; cover and chill
- Prepare a pumpkin drink holder

30 minutes before:

- Prepare Mummy Dogs
- Pipe border on lollipops, and attach ribbon
- Prepare apples for bobbing
- Chill drinks

Just before serving:

- Attach stem, vine, and leaf to cheese ball
- Prepare ketchup and mustard for hot dogs

Pumpkin Cheese Ball

makes 15 appetizer servings   hands-on time: 15 min. **total time: 15 min.**

1 (10-oz.) block extra-sharp white
    Cheddar cheese, shredded
1 (10-oz.) block extra-sharp Cheddar
    cheese, shredded
1 (8-oz.) package cream cheese, softened

2 (4-oz.) goat cheese logs, softened
½ tsp. pepper
Braided pretzel, muscadine vine and leaf
Crackers and assorted vegetables

1. Stir together first 5 ingredients. Shape mixture into a ball to resemble a pumpkin. Smooth pumpkin's entire surface with metal spatula or table knife. Make vertical grooves in ball, if desired, using fingertips. Press pretzel into top of cheese ball to resemble a pumpkin stem; place muscadine vine and leaf beside pretzel. Serve with crackers and assorted vegetables.

Note: We tested with Cracker Barrel Extra Sharp Cheddar Cheese.

Make Ahead Note: To make ahead, wrap cheese ball in plastic wrap, without stem, vine, or leaf, and store in refrigerator up to two days. Attach stem, vine, and leaf before serving.

hip tip Halve and hollow out a pumpkin, add copper piping to resemble spider legs, and then fill it with ice and drinks for an inventive **cooler**.

fast flourish Drag a wooden pick through a bowl of mustard and ketchup to create the **web design**.

Mummy Dogs

makes 12 servings   hands-on time: 10 min.   **total time: 30 min.**

1 (11-oz.) can refrigerated breadstick dough
12 bun-length hot dogs
Wooden picks (optional)

Vegetable cooking spray
Ketchup
Mustard

1. Preheat oven to 400°. Unroll breadstick dough, and separate into 12 strips at perforations. Gently stretch each strip to a length of 8 inches. Wrap 1 dough strip lengthwise around each hot dog. Secure with wooden picks, if necessary. Coat lightly with cooking spray. Place on a lightly greased baking sheet.

2. Bake at 400° for 15 minutes or until golden brown. Let stand 5 minutes. (If using wooden picks, remove before serving.) Serve with ketchup and mustard.

Garlic Mummy Dogs: Substitute 1 (11-oz.) can refrigerated garlic breadstick dough. Proceed with recipe as directed.

Parmesan-Garlic Mummy Dogs: Substitute 1 (11-oz.) can refrigerated Parmesan-garlic breadstick dough. Proceed with recipe as directed.

Garlic-Herb Mummy Dogs: Substitute 1 (11-oz.) can refrigerated garlic-herb breadstick dough. Proceed with recipe as directed.

Harvest Moon Lollipops

makes 12 lollipops   hands-on time: 30 min.   **total time: 30 min.,** not including standing

These make a perfect party project for kids. (Help younger children insert the lollipop sticks.) Arrange lollipops in a container filled with florist foam for a centerpiece, or give them as party favors.

12 (10- to 12-inch-long) lollipop sticks
1 (24-oz.) package chocolate-marshmallow
    sandwich cookies
1 (14-oz.) package orange candy melts
Wax paper

Halloween candies
Halloween sugar cake decorations
Decorator icing
Ribbon (optional)

1. Insert 1 lollipop stick 2 to 3 inches into marshmallow center of each chocolate sandwich cookie.

2. Microwave candy melts in a glass bowl at MEDIUM (50%) power 1 minute or until melted, stirring once; spoon melted candy into a zip-top plastic bag, and seal.

3. Snip 1 corner of bag to make a small hole; pipe melted candy around where sticks meet sandwich cookies to secure. Lay flat on wax paper, and let stand until firm (about 30 minutes).

4. Pipe melted candy around edges of cookies. Attach candies and cake decorations to cookies using decorator icing. Tie ribbons around sticks, if desired.

Note: We tested with MoonPie chocolate marshmallow sandwich cookies.

just for the kids

menu

serves 10

Fruit Skewers with Strawberry Dip

Turkey Roll-ups

Reindeer Food

Elf Cookies

egg nog

Host a holiday party for your favorite pint-size people at home or in the school classroom before winter break. Bite-size treats are fun to eat, and this celebration is a wonderful way to stir up a little Christmas cheer during the most magical season of all.

hostess
hit list:

Promote caring and sharing this joyous time of year. Choose a charity in advance and have the kids bring a wrapped gift to give others.

The day before:

- Prepare Turkey Roll-ups; cover and chill
- Prepare Reindeer Food; store in an airtight container
- Prepare Elf Cookies; store in an airtight container

 ### 30 minutes before:

- Prepare fruit skewers

15 minutes before:

- Set up party

Just before serving:

- Place menu items in serving pieces

Fruit Skewers with Strawberry Dip

makes 12 servings   hands-on time: 20 min.   **total time: 20 min.**

Make skewers up to 3 hours before the party. The pineapple juice keeps the apples from turning brown.

¼ cup pineapple juice
1   medium-size Braeburn apple, cut into
    12 small chunks
1   medium-size Granny Smith apple, cut into
    12 small chunks
12 seedless red grapes

12 seedless green grapes
12 large fresh strawberries, halved
12 (6-inch) wooden skewers*
2   (6-oz.) containers strawberry cheesecake-flavored
    yogurt

1. Combine pineapple juice and 2 Tbsp. water in a large bowl. Add apple chunks to bowl, tossing to coat.

2. Thread 1 Braeburn and Granny Smith apple piece, 1 red and green grape, and 2 strawberry halves onto each skewer. Serve fruit skewers with yogurt for dipping.

*Plastic coffee stirrers may be substituted if the points of wooden skewers are a concern for young children.

Note: We tested with Yoplait Original Strawberry Cheesecake 99% Fat Free Yogurt.

Turkey Roll-ups

makes 26 roll-ups   hands-on time: 11 min.   **total time: 11 min.**

8   thin white American cheese slices
26 thinly sliced deli smoked turkey slices (about 1 lb.)

8   thin orange American cheese slices
1   (8-oz.) container cream cheese, softened

1. Place 1 white American cheese slice on 1 turkey slice; roll up tightly, and place, seam side down, on a cutting board. Repeat procedure with 15 turkey slices, orange American cheese slices, and remaining white American cheese slices.

2. Spread about 1 Tbsp. cream cheese onto each of remaining 10 turkey slices; roll up. Reserve remaining cream cheese for another use. Cut roll-ups in half diagonally, if desired. Arrange roll-ups on a serving platter. Cover and chill up to 24 hours.

Note: We tested with Sara Lee deli smoked turkey.

Reindeer Food

makes 20 servings   hands-on time: 6 min.   **total time: 26 min.**

This crispy, sweet snack mix is the perfect party favor or teacher gift.

1 ½ cups semisweet chocolate morsels

½   cup hazelnut spread

10 cups corn-and-rice cereal

2   cups powdered sugar

2   cups candy-coated chocolate pieces

1. Microwave chocolate morsels and hazelnut spread in a medium-size, microwave-safe bowl at HIGH 1 minute or until melted, stirring at 30-second intervals.

2. Place cereal in a large bowl. Pour chocolate mixture over cereal; toss well to coat. Add powdered sugar, and toss to coat. Stir in candy pieces. Let cool 20 minutes. Store candy mixture in an airtight container up to 1 week.

Note: We tested with Nutella Hazelnut Spread, Crispix Cereal, and M&M's Chocolate Pieces.

fast flourish An inexpensive holiday cup-and-saucer set filled with snack mix is a tasty and memorable takeaway keepsake.

Elf Cookies

makes 10 cookies   **hands-on time: 15 min.**   **total time: 25 min.,** not including cooling time

Set up a cookie decorating station during the party, and let the kids create these whimsical faces. Bake the cookies the day before.

1   (16.5-oz.) package sugar cookie dough
½   cup all-purpose flour
Parchment paper
1   egg white, lightly beaten

Red and green decorator sugar crystals
1   (4.25-oz.) tube white decorating icing
20   milk chocolate or semisweet chocolate morsels

1. Preheat oven to 350°. Combine cookie dough and flour; knead with hands until blended. Roll dough to ¼-inch thickness on a lightly floured surface.

2. Cut dough using an elf-shaped cookie cutter. Reroll scraps as needed.

3. Place cutouts 1 inch apart on large, parchment paper-lined baking sheets. Brush hats and bowties of elves with egg white; sprinkle with decorator sugar crystals.

4. Bake at 350° for 10 to 12 minutes or until edges are lightly browned. Cool on baking sheets 5 minutes; remove from baking sheets to wire racks, and cool completely (about 20 minutes).

5. Pipe 2 drops of icing onto each cookie for eyes. Top each with a chocolate morsel.

Note: We tested with Betty Crocker White Frosting and Pillsbury Sugar Cookie Dough Sheets. Find sugar cookie dough sheets in the dairy case of your grocery store during the holiday season.

how to stock a bar

Plan Ahead

Add cheer to any party with a well-planned bar. Store spirits on a tray that slides easily in and out of your liquor cabinet for a grab-and-go setup. Make note of what needs replenishing after every party, and purchase it before you need it so that you are always prepared.

The Basics

A great party doesn't require an extensive bar offering or even an exotic one. Simply put, you must make sure that you can supply all the basic ingredients required for your guests' drinks. Covering the basics just takes advanced planning and some simple math to determine the amounts needed.

Make It Pretty

Instead of the standard white tablecloth-covered card table, go the extra mile. For pizzazz, drape the table with brightly colored fabric, or use a vintage bar cart for a more retro serving station. Dress up drinks with fruit-juice ice cubes or colored salt and sugar rims. Serve wine from pretty decanters rather than directly from the bottle.

Place a fresh flower arrangement on the bar. Offer wine glass charms or beer bands to help guests remember whose cocktail is whose, and set out napkins to prevent drink rings on furniture. Identify premixed or decanted drinks with decorative labels to let guests know what is what. Plan ahead and order custom-designed koozies that guests can take home at the end of the night. Our favorite, spotted at a couple's engagement cookout, read, "To have and to hold and to keep your beer cold."

The Well-Stocked Bar

The list below includes the most commonly requested elixirs. Build your inventory with Italian Campari, French Pernod, or Brazilian cachaça if you find yourself a budding mixologist.

gin	whiskey	tequila
Scotch	rum	bourbon
vodka	vermouth	bottled beer
wine *(red and white)*		

Mixers:

cola	ginger ale	club soda
tonic	cranberry juice	orange juice
simple syrup *(for sweetening cocktails)*	tomato juice *(for Bloody Mary mix)*	

The Accoutrements

These are the most commonly used tools and flourishes.

martini shaker	corkscrew	ice
ice bucket	blender	large ice chest/cooler
napkins		

Bar Flair:

stirrers	tiny umbrellas	wine glass charms
cocktail toothpicks		

Garnishes:

olives	lemons	citrus twists
limes	cherries	caper berries
mint sprigs	oranges	salt and sanding sugar *(for glass rims)*

Glasses:

shot glasses	wine glasses	pilsners
martini glasses	champagne flutes	highball glasses
double old-fashioned glasses		

Glasses, Cups, etc.

Plastic cups, crystal stemware, and ruby-tinted martini glasses are all okay depending on the style, theme, and time of your party. If your party is formal, opt for crystal. If it's a barbecue, choose plastic. Traditionally, white and red wines are served in different types of glasses (narrower for whites, wider for reds so that they can breathe). However, there is no actual rule requiring you to serve beverages in any certain type of glass, but offering a selection of glasses will add more sophistication to your bar. Stock up on inexpensive sets of a variety of wine glasses, martini glasses, pilsners, and Champagne flutes that you store for festive occasions, and consider sharing the cost and use with a friend.

If you're hosting a casual barbecue, pick up funky, plastic margarita and martini glasses at local stores for about $1–$3 each. It's okay if they're mismatched—you're going for a casual look. For a more elegant affair, rent high-quality glass stemware from a party rental store. They'll cost around $1 per stem for the night, and you won't have to do any hand washing or worry about chipping your own crystal.

Ice Advice

A good rule of thumb for any party is to have anywhere between a half pound to one pound of ice per person. That may sound like a lot, but remember that you may need ice to fill an ice chest on the back porch, to blend with frozen mixes, and to serve cocktails on the rocks.

Buy bags of ice and store them in an ice chest on the deck, or, for smaller parties, empty the ice from your freezer's ice maker into an extra container in your freezer the night before to allow double ice storing and production capacity. Ice typically comes in five-pound bags; determine how many bags you will need before you head to the store. Don't forget to put a cooler in your car to keep your ice frozen solid.

Estimating Pours

Purchase at least half a bottle of wine per person for any gathering, but err on the generous side. Think about how your event is planned. Is it a sit-down dinner party or a reception? Adjust drink expectations accordingly. A standard bottle has about five 5-ounce servings, so we suggest 4 glasses for brunch (1 for appetizers, 2 for entrée, 1 for dessert), 3 to 4 glasses for a cocktail party, 1 bottle per person for an evening buffet, and 6 glasses for a dinner party (2 glasses for appetizers, 3 for entrée, and 1 for dessert). Half a bottle per person may sound like a lot, but remember that you know your guests best. Buy more or less depending on your crowd.

Popping the Cork

If you're serving only red and white wine, make sure there's enough of each and that they're at the right temperature. Chill white wines in the fridge or a wine chiller. Open red wines early to allow them to breathe. Two things to keep in mind about wine: Red keeps well, so don't worry about over-purchasing, and retailers may allow you to return unopened, unchilled white wines. When pouring, fill glasses just under the halfway mark.

Signature Cocktails

Special concoctions mixed to fit the theme of the party are another way to give your personal stamp to an affair. Typically, they are mixed-liquor drinks, but they can also be a special beer or a nonalcoholic drink. It may seem like extra work, but their special presentation will add an extra dimension to your festivities. See the *Half-Hour Hostess's* favorite recipes beginning on the following page.

Personalize it. If you don't like gin, then substitute vodka. Give the drink a sassy name, such as "Sally's Send-Away Sangria" for a farewell party, or a "Movingtini" martini for a housewarming event. Serve the libation in a special glass with decorative garnishes (umbrellas, drink stirrers, etc). Be sure to have a large pitcher of the drink on hand so that guests can refill themselves.

classic cocktail
recipes and mixers

Classic Martini

makes 1 serving   hands-on time: 5 min.   total time: 5 min.

The secret is to chill everything except the vermouth in the freezer before you start. To make a dirty martini, increase the olive juice by a few tablespoons.

Crushed ice
3   Tbsp. vermouth
½   cup vodka

3   Tbsp. Spanish olive brine or juice
Large pimiento-stuffed Spanish olive

1. Fill a cocktail shaker with crushed ice. Add vermouth; cover with lid, and shake until thoroughly chilled. Discard vermouth, reserving ice in shaker. Add vodka and Spanish olive brine to ice in shaker; cover with lid, and shake until thoroughly chilled (about 30 seconds). Pour into a chilled martini glass. Serve immediately with a large pimiento-stuffed Spanish olive.

Gin and Tonic

makes 1 serving   hands-on time: 5 min.   total time: 5 min.

1   oz. (2 Tbsp.) gin*
⅓   cup tonic

1 ½ tsp. freshly squeezed lime juice
Lime wedges

1. Fill a highball glass with ice, and top with gin, tonic, and lime juice. Stir; serve with lime wedges.
*Vodka may be substituted.

Manhattan

makes 1 serving   hands-on time: 5 min.   total time: 5 min.

1 ½ oz. whiskey or bourbon
½ oz. sweet vermouth

Maraschino cherry
Orange slice

1. Fill a cocktail shaker with ice, and add whiskey and vermouth; shake.
2. Strain into a glass, without ice, to serve straight up. Or strain into glass, with ice, to serve "on the rocks."
Garnish with a cherry and slice of orange.
Dry Manhattan: Substitute dry vermouth for sweet vermouth.

Classic Margarita

makes 1 serving   hands-on time: 10 min.   total time: 10 min.

Fresh lime wedge (optional)
Margarita salt (optional)
⅓ cup fresh lime juice
3 Tbsp. orange liqueur

2 Tbsp. tequila
⅓ to ½ cup powdered sugar
Garnish: lime slice

1. Rub rim of a chilled margarita glass with lime wedge, and dip rim in salt to coat, if desired.
2. Fill cocktail shaker half full with ice. Add lime juice, liqueur, tequila, and powdered sugar; cover with lid, and shake until thoroughly chilled. Strain into prepared glass. Garnish, if desired, and serve immediately.
Shortcut Margarita: Substitute ⅓ cup thawed frozen limeade concentrate for fresh lime juice. Omit powdered sugar, and proceed with recipe as directed.

Mojito

makes 1 serving   hands-on time: 5 min.   total time: 5 min.

This is Cuba's signature libation. A frequent visitor to the tropics, Ernest Hemingway named this his beverage of choice.

10 fresh mint leaves
2 Tbsp. sugar
Juice from ½ lime (about 2 Tbsp.)

¼ cup light rum
Splash of club soda

1. Combine mint leaves, sugar, and lime juice in a highball glass; crush mint using the back of a spoon.
2. Add rum, and stir; add ice cubes. Add a splash of club soda.

metric equivalents

The recipes that appear in this cookbook use the standard U.S. method for measuring liquid and dry or solid ingredients (teaspoons, tablespoons, and cups). The information in the following charts is provided to help cooks outside the United States successfully use these recipes. All equivalents are approximate.

Metric Equivalents for Different Types of Ingredients

A standard cup measure of a dry or solid ingredient will vary in weight depending on the type of ingredient. A standard cup of liquid is the same volume for any type of liquid. Use the following chart when converting standard cup measures to grams (weight) or milliliters (volume).

Standard Cup	Fine Powder (ex. flour)	Grain (ex. rice)	Granular (ex. sugar)	Liquid Solids (ex. butter)	Liquid (ex. milk)
1	140 g	150 g	190 g	200 g	240 ml
¾	105 g	113 g	143 g	150 g	180 ml
⅔	93 g	100 g	125 g	133 g	160 ml
½	70 g	75 g	95 g	100 g	120 ml
⅓	47 g	50 g	63 g	67 g	80 ml
¼	35 g	38 g	48 g	50 g	60 ml
⅛	18 g	19 g	24 g	25 g	30 ml

Useful Equivalents for Liquid Ingredients by Volume

¼ tsp					=	1 ml		
½ tsp					=	2 ml		
1 tsp					=	5 ml		
3 tsp	=	1 Tbsp		=	½ fl oz	=	15 ml	
		2 Tbsp	= ⅛ cup	=	1 fl oz	=	30 ml	
		4 Tbsp	= ¼ cup	=	2 fl oz	=	60 ml	
		5⅓ Tbsp	= ⅓ cup	=	3 fl oz	=	80 ml	
		8 Tbsp	= ½ cup	=	4 fl oz	=	120 ml	
		10⅔ Tbsp	= ⅔ cup	=	5 fl oz	=	160 ml	
		12 Tbsp	= ¾ cup	=	6 fl oz	=	180 ml	
		16 Tbsp	= 1 cup	=	8 fl oz	=	240 ml	
	1 pt	= 2 cups		=	16 fl oz	=	480 ml	= 1 l
	1 qt	= 4 cups		=	32 fl oz	=	960 ml	
					33 fl oz	=	1000 ml	

Useful Equivalents for Dry Ingredients by Weight

(To convert ounces to grams, multiply the number of ounces by 30.)

1 oz	=	⅟₁₆ lb	=	30 g
4 oz	=	¼ lb	=	120 g
8 oz	=	½ lb	=	240 g
12 oz	=	¾ lb	=	360 g
16 oz	=	1 lb	=	480 g

Useful Equivalents for Length

(To convert inches to centimeters, multiply the number of inches by 2.5.)

1 in				=	2.5 cm		
6 in	=	½ ft		=	15 cm		
12 in	=	1 ft		=	30 cm		
36 in	=	3 ft	= 1 yd	=	90 cm		
40 in				=	100 cm	=	1 m

Useful Equivalents for Cooking/Oven Temperatures

	Fahrenheit	Celsius	Gas Mark
Freeze water	32° F	0° C	
Room temperature	68° F	20° C	
Boil water	212° F	100° C	
Bake	325° F	160° C	3
	350° F	180° C	4
	375° F	190° C	5
	400° F	200° C	6
	425° F	220° C	7
	450° F	230° C	8
Broil			Grill

index